Also edited by Carmela Ciuraru

BEAT POETS

FIRST LOVES:
*Poets Introduce the Essential Poems
That Captivated & Inspired Them*

POEMS *for* AMERICA

125 POEMS THAT CELEBRATE
THE AMERICAN EXPERIENCE

EDITED BY

Carmela Ciuraru

SCRIBNER POETRY
New York   London   Toronto   Sydney   Singapore

SCRIBNER POETRY
1230 Avenue of the Americas
New York, NY 10020

SCRIBNER POETRY and design are trademarks of Macmillan Library Reference USA, Inc.,
used under license by Simon & Schuster, the publisher of this work.

For information about special discounts for bulk purchases,
please contact Simon & Schuster Special Sales:
1-800-456-6798 or business@simonandschuster.com

DESIGNED BY ERICH HOBBING

Manufactured in the United States of America

1   3   5   7   9   10   8   6   4   2

Library of Congress Cataloging-in-Publication Data is available.

ISBN 0-7432-4486-9

In memory of my mother and father

ACKNOWLEDGMENTS

My gratitude to Tina Bennett, Gillian Blake, Timothy Donnelly, Rory Evans, Sarah Fitzharding, Devon Hodges, Barbara Jones, Deborah Kaplan, Alice Quinn, Rachel Sussman, and Elaine Valby.

I like to be in America!
O.K. by me in America!
Ev'rything free in America!
For a small fee in America!
—Stephen Sondheim

America?
An international river with a legion of tributaries!
A magnificent cosmorama with myriad patterns and colors!
A giant forest with loin-roots in a hundred lands!
A cosmopolitan orchestra with a thousand instruments playing
America!
—Melvin B. Tolson

Wait Mister. Which way is home?
—Anne Sexton

CONTENTS

POEMS *for* AMERICA

INTRODUCTION

I came to America when I was six months old. My parents had left Romania for Israel and then Canada, where I was born, arriving finally in the United States. As a child I could not understand why they had abandoned their home country for one where they knew no one and could not speak the native language. One day I asked my father about what life had been like in Romania. "It was terrible there," he said. I could tell that he didn't want to say much else. Neither did my mother. They became American citizens the year they were eligible to do so, grateful for the opportunities and freedom they found in their adopted country.

Although for most of my life I have taken patriotism for granted—one of the many privileges of being American—while working on this project, I repeatedly thought about it . For me, patriotism resonates most deeply when I consider the American art and music and literature so essential to my enjoyment of life. Poetry has been especially important, and as I compiled the selections for this anthology, I was again astonished by the range of verse the United States has produced.

Our poetry is defined by daring and diversity, virtues that have historically defined the nation itself. In the early nineteenth century, the poetry of America left the visiting Frenchman Alexis de Tocqueville exceedingly unimpressed, though optimistic about its future. "I readily admit that the Americans have no poets," he wrote in *Democracy in America*. "Nothing conceivable is so petty, so insipid, so crowded with paltry interests—in one word, so antipoetic—as the life of a man in the United States." He asserted that Americans preferred achieving greater wealth to indulging in literary and artistic pursuits. A love of wealth, he wrote, was "to be traced, as either a principal or an accessory motive, at the bottom of all that the Americans do; this gives to all their passions a sort of family likeness and soon renders the survey of them exceedingly wearisome."

Tocqueville's assessment of our materialism and "garrulous" patriotic zeal was astute (and would seem to hold true, nearly two hundred years later), but if he were to revisit the United States today, it's likely that he would appreciate the scope of our nation's poets, whose dazzling experiments and innovations resist categorization. A survey of American poetry reveals a prodigious array of visions, rhythms, voices, and stylistic feats. From Walt Whitman's soaring arias to the elegant, mysterious musings of Wallace Stevens, the broken-down cries of John Berryman, and the casual ebullience of Frank O'Hara, our poets have established traditions and then consistently shattered and reinvented them. Yet the ecstasy conveyed in American poetry has been a constant, reflecting the country's vast and energetic spirit. "The United States themselves are essentially the greatest poem," Whitman wrote in his preface to *Leaves of Grass*.

When our country has experienced profound turmoil, poets have provided words to edify and console us. This was especially true in the aftermath of September 11, 2001. In *Poems for America,* none of the selections address the ineffable horror of September 11, but in a subtle way, William Matthews' brief poem "Why We Are Truly a Nation," written years before that tragedy occurred, can be read as a response to it: "Because we rage inside," he writes. "Because grief unites us."

A number of poems in this volume chronicle our nation's history through moving personal narratives of domestic duties, church-going, farm work, urban travels, and wartime anxieties. They offer vivid scenes of American life, from the seventeenth century (beginning with Anne Bradstreet's "Here Follows Some Verses Upon the Burning of Our House July 10, 1666. Copied Out of a Loose Paper") through the late twentieth century (Sherman Alexie's "At the Navajo Monument Valley Tribal School"). Of course, this history-via-poetry is subjective and therefore incomplete. As the poet Hayden Carruth lamented in the foreword to his twentieth-century poetry anthology *The Voice That Is Great Within Us,* "An anthology at best is a system of compromises, because its field of interest is inevitably too big to be encompassed by its physical limits."

In seeking poetry that captured quintessentially American experiences, I was led on occasion to poems that may not be representative of a poet's work as a whole, but that convey some distinctive American quality. This produced an unexpected mix of classics—such as John Greenleaf Whittier's "Barbara Frietchie" and Ralph Waldo Emerson's "Concord Hymn"—and lesser-known works by poets such as Amy Lowell, Carl Sandburg, and William Carlos Williams.

Some of the most harrowing and beautiful poems about the American experience have been written by African-American poets. In this volume, the evolution of African-American poetry can be traced, from what the late poet Gwendolyn Brooks described in *A Capsule Course in Black Poetry Writing* as the "cautious imitations" of Phillis Wheatley, the first published African-American poet, to the "burning braveries" of George Moses Horton, the "hard and heady incense" of Claude McKay, and the "pioneering geniality and blackness-warmth" of Langston Hughes. Over time, poetry by African-Americans developed into work that "italicizes black identity, black solidarity, black self-possession and self-address," wrote Brooks. Such progress is evident in her own poetry, and in the work of poets like Ishmael Reed, Sonia Sanchez, Nikki Giovanni, and many others not included here.

Although experiences of racism, deprivation, and exclusion are described throughout this collection—they are a fact of American existence—many of the poems express jubilation and nostalgia. "It is a noble country where we dwell," declares Thoreau in "Our Country." He goes on: "Look nearer,—know the lineaments of each face,—/ Learn the far-travelled race, and find here met / The so long gathering congress of the world!" Or in Richard Wilbur's lovely and intimate "Wellfleet: The House": "The sea strokes up to fashion dune and beach / In strew by strew, and year by hundred years. / One is at home here. Nowhere in ocean's reach / Can time have any foreignness or fears."

Other poets offer more complicated perspectives of America, and eloquently acknowledge that the task of honoring this country is not an easy one. Their apprehension is often overcome by feelings of tenderness and pride. "War and secrecy / make writing America / a twistsome thing," writes Edward Sanders in his poem "Introduction," which serves as this anthology's Afterword. He admits to having shaken his head thousands of times "with the ghastly sudden knowledge / of this and that." Yet he concludes the poem by asking "how many thousands more / have I smiled at the millions / who have made my nation a marvel."

Here, then, is a journey through more than three hundred years of this marvel.

Carmela Ciuraru
New York City

3

Here Follows Some Verses
upon the Burning of Our House July 10th, 1666.
Copied Out of a Loose Paper

In silent night when rest I took
For sorrow near I did not look
I wakened was with thund'ring noise
And piteous shrieks of dreadful voice.
That fearful sound of "Fire!" and "Fire!"
Let no man know is my desire.
I, starting up, the light did spy,
And to my God my heart did cry
To strengthen me in my distress
And not to leave me succorless.
Then, coming out, beheld a space
The flame consume my dwelling place.
And when I could no longer look,
I blest His name that gave and took,
That laid my goods now in the dust.
Yea, so it was, and so 'twas just.
It was His own, it was not mine,
Far be it that I should repine;
He might of all justly bereft
But yet sufficient for us left.
When by the ruins oft I past
My sorrowing eyes aside did cast,
And here and there the places spy
Where oft I sat and long did lie:
Here stood that trunk, and there that chest,

There lay that store I counted best.
My pleasant things in ashes lie,
And them behold no more shall I.
Under thy roof no guest shall sit,
Nor at thy table eat a bit.
No pleasant tale shall e'er be told,
Nor things recounted done of old.
No candle e'er shall shine in thee,
Nor bridegroom's voice e'er heard shall be.
In silence ever shall thou lie,
Adieu, Adieu, all's vanity.
Then straight I 'gin my heart to chide,
And did thy wealth on earth abide?
Didst fix thy hope on mold'ring dust?
The arm of flesh didst make thy trust?
Raise up thy thoughts above the sky
That dunghill mists away may fly.
Thou hast an house on high erect,
Framed by that mighty Architect,
With glory richly furnished,
Stands permanent though this be fled.
It's purchased and paid for too
By Him who hath enough to do.
A price so vast as is unknown
Yet by His gift is made thine own;
There's wealth enough, I need no more,
Farewell, my pelf, farewell my store.
The world no longer let me love,
My hope and treasure lies above.

—*Anne Bradstreet*

The Indian Burying Ground

In spite of all the learned have said,
I still my old opinion keep;
The *posture,* that *we* give the dead,
Points out the soul's eternal sleep.

Not so the ancients of these lands—
The Indian, when from life released,
Again is seated with his friends,
And shares again the joyous feast.

His imaged birds, and painted bowl,
And venison, for a journey dressed,
Bespeak the nature of the soul,
ACTIVITY, that knows no rest.

His bow, for action ready bent,
And arrows, with a head of stone,
Can only mean that life is spent,
And not the old ideas gone.

Thou, stranger, that shalt come this way,
No fraud upon the dead commit—
Observe the swelling turf, and say
They do not *lie,* but here they *sit.*

Here still a lofty rock remains,
On which the curious eye may trace

(Now wasted, half, by wearing rains)
The fancies of a ruder race.

Here still an aged elm aspires,
Beneath whose far-projecting shade
(And which the shepherd still admires)
The children of the forest played!

There oft a restless Indian queen
(Pale *Shebah,* with her braided hair)
And many a barbarous form is seen
To chide the man that lingers there.

By midnight moons, o'er moistening dews,
In habit for the chase arrayed,
The hunter still the deer pursues,
The hunter and the deer, a shade!

And long shall timorous fancy see
The painted chief, and pointed spear,
And Reason's self shall bow the knee
To shadows and delusions here.

—Philip Freneau

To the Right Honourable William, Earl of Dartmouth, His Majesty's Principal Secretary of State for North America, &c.

Hail, happy day, when, smiling like the morn,
Fair *Freedom* rose *New-England* to adorn:
The northern clime beneath her genial ray,
Dartmouth, congratulates thy blissful sway:
Elate with hope her race no longer mourns,
Each soul expands, each grateful bosom burns,
While in thine hand with pleasure we behold
The silken reins, and *Freedom's* charms unfold.
Long lost to realms beneath the northern skies
She shines supreme, while hated *faction* dies:
Soon as appear'd the *Goddess* long desir'd,
Sick at the view, she lanquish'd and expir'd;
Thus from the splendors of the morning light
The owl in sadness seeks the caves of night.

    No more, *America,* in mournful strain
Of wrongs, and grievance unredress'd complain,
No longer shalt thou dread the iron chain,
Which wanton *Tyranny* with lawless hand
Had made, and with it meant t' enslave the land.

    Should you, my lord, while you peruse my song,
Wonder from whence my love of *Freedom* sprung,
Whence flow these wishes for the common good,
By feeling hearts alone best understood,

I, young in life, by seeming cruel fate
Was snatch'd from *Afric's* fancy'd happy seat:
What pangs excruciating must molest,
What sorrows labour in my parent's breast?
Steel'd was that soul and by no misery mov'd
That from a father seiz'd his babe belov'd:
Such, such my case. And can I then but pray
Others may never feel tyrannic sway?

    For favours past, great Sir, our thanks are due,
And thee we ask thy favours to renew,
Since in thy pow'r, as in thy will before,
To sooth the griefs, which thou did'st once deplore.
May heav'nly grace the sacred sanction give
To all thy works, and thou for ever live
Not only on the wings of fleeting *Fame,*
Though praise immortal crowns the patriot's name,
But to conduct to heav'ns refulgent fane,
May fiery coursers sweep th' ethereal plain,
And bear thee upwards to that blest abode,
Where, like the prophet, thou shalt find thy God.

—*Phillis Wheatley*

To a Lady on Her Remarkable Preservation in an Hurricane in North Carolina

Though thou did'st hear the tempest from afar,
And felt'st the horrors of the wat'ry war,
To me unknown, yet on this peaceful shore
Methinks I hear the storm tumultuous roar,
And how stern *Boreas* with impetuous hand
Compell'd the *Nereids* to usurp the land.
Reluctant rose the daughters of the main,
And flow ascending glided o'er the plain,
Till *Æolus* in his rapid chariot drove
In gloomy grandeur from the vault above:
Furious he comes. His winged sons obey
Their frantic fire, and madden all the sea
The billows rave, the wind's fierce tyrant roars,
And with his thund'ring terrors shakes the shores.
Broken by waves the vessel's frame is rent,
And strows with planks the wat'ry element.

But thee, *Maria,* a kind *Nereid's* shield
Preserv'd from sinking, and thy form upheld:
And sure some heav'nly oracle design'd
At that dread crisis to instruct thy mind
Things of eternal consequence to weigh,
And to thine heart just feelings to convey
Of things above, and of the future doom,
And what the births of the dread worlds to come.

From tossing seas I welcome thee to land.
"Resign her, *Nereid,*" 'twas thy God's command.
Thy spouse late buried, as thy fears conceiv'd,
Again returns, thy fears are all reliev'd:
Thy daughter blooming with superior grace
Again thou see'st, again thine arms embrace;
O come, and joyful show thy spouse his heir,
And what the blessings of maternal care!

—*Phillis Wheatley*

The Indian's Welcome
to the Pilgrim Fathers

Above them spread a stranger sky;
    Around, the sterile plain;
The rock-bound coast rose frowning nigh;
    Beyond,—the wrathful main:
Chill remnants of the wintry snow
    Still chok'd the encumber'd soil,
Yet forth these Pilgrim Fathers go
    To mark their future toil.

'Mid yonder vale their corn must rise
    In summer's ripening pride,
And there the church-spire woo the skies
    Its sister-school beside.
Perchance 'mid England's velvet green
    Some tender thought repos'd,
Though nought upon their stoic mien
    Such soft regret disclos'd.

When sudden from the forest wide
    A red-brow'd chieftain came,
With towering form, and haughty stride,
    And eye like kindling flame:
No wrath he breath'd, no conflict sought,
    To no dark ambush drew,
But simply to the Old World brought,
    The welcome of the New.

That welcome was a blast and ban
    Upon thy race unborn;
Was there no seer,—thou fated Man!
    Thy lavish zeal to warn?
Thou in thy fearless faith didst hail
    A weak, invading band,
But who shall heed thy children's wail,
    Swept from their native land?

Thou gav'st the riches of thy streams,
    The lordship o'er thy waves,
The region of thine infant dreams,
    And of thy fathers' graves,—
But who to yon proud mansions pil'd
    With wealth of earth and sea,
Poor outcast from thy forest wild,
    Say, who shall welcome thee?

—Lydia Huntley Sigourney

Excerpt, The Prairies

These are the gardens of the Desert, these
The unshorn fields, boundless and beautiful,
For which the speech of England has no name—
The Prairies. I behold them for the first,
And my heart swells, while the dilated sight
Takes in the encircling vastness. Lo! they stretch,
In airy undulations, far away,
As if the ocean, in his gentlest swell,
Stood still, with all his rounded billows fixed,
And motionless forever.—Motionless?—
No—they are all unchained again. The clouds
Sweep over with their shadows, and, beneath,
The surface rolls and fluctuates to the eye;
Dark hollows seem to glide along and chase
The sunny ridges. Breezes of the South!
Who toss the golden and the flame-like flowers,
And pass the prairie-hawk that, poised on high,
Flaps his broad wings, yet moves not—ye have played
Among the palms of Mexico and vines
Of Texas, and have crisped the limpid brooks
That from the fountains of Sonora glide
Into the calm Pacific—have ye fanned
A nobler or a lovelier scene than this?
Man hath no power in all this glorious work:
The hand that built the firmament hath heaved
And smoothed these verdant swells, and sown their slopes
With herbage, planted them with island groves,
And hedged them round with forests. Fitting floor

For this magnificent temple of the sky—
With flowers whose glory and whose multitude
Rival the constellations! The great heavens
Seem to stoop down upon the scene in love,—
A nearer vault, and of a tenderer blue,
Than that which bends above our eastern hills.

—*William Cullen Bryant*

On Liberty and Slavery

Alas! and am I born for this,
    To wear this slavish chain?
Deprived of all created bliss,
    Through hardship, toil and pain!

How long have I in bondage lain,
    And languished to be free!
Alas! and must I still complain—
    Deprived of liberty.

Oh, Heaven! and is there no relief
    This side the silent grave—
To soothe the pain—to quell the grief
    And anguish of a slave?

Come Liberty, thou cheerful sound,
    Roll through my ravished ears!
Come, let my grief in joys be drowned,
    And drive away my fears.

Say unto foul oppression, Cease:
    Ye tyrants rage no more,
And let the joyful trump of peace,
    Now bid the vassal soar.

Soar on the pinions of that dove
    Which long has cooed for thee,

And breathed her notes from Afric's grove,
    The sound of Liberty.

Oh, Liberty! thou golden prize,
    So often sought by blood—
We crave thy sacred sun to rise,
    The gift of nature's God!

Bid Slavery hide her haggard face,
    And barbarism fly:
I scorn to see the sad disgrace
    In which enslaved I lie.

Dear Liberty! upon thy breast,
    I languish to respire;
And like the Swan unto her nest,
    I'd to thy smiles retire.

Oh, blest asylum—heavenly balm!
    Unto thy boughs I flee—
And in thy shades the storm shall calm,
    With songs of Liberty!

—*George Moses Horton*

The New-England Boy's Song
About Thanksgiving Day

Over the river, and through the wood,
  To grandfather's house we go;
    The horse knows the way,
    To carry the sleigh,
  Through the white and drifted snow.

Over the river, and through the wood,
  To grandfather's house away!
    We would not stop
    For doll or top,
  For 't is Thanksgiving day.

Over the river, and through the wood,
  Oh, how the wind does blow!
    It stings the toes,
    And bites the nose,
  As over the ground we go.

Over the river, and through the wood,
  With a clear blue winter sky,
    The dogs do bark,
    And children hark,
  As we go jingling by.

Over the river, and through the wood,
  To have a first-rate play—

Hear the bells ring
Ting a ling ding,
Hurra for Thanksgiving day!

Over the river, and through the wood—
No matter for winds that blow;
Or if we get
The sleigh upset,
Into a bank of snow.

Over the river, and through the wood,
To see little John and Ann;
We will kiss them all,
And play snow-ball,
And stay as long as we can.

Over the river, and through the wood,
Trot fast, my dapple grey!
Spring over the ground,
Like a hunting hound,
For 't is Thanksgiving day!

Over the river, and through the wood,
And straight through the barn-yard gate;
We seem to go
Extremely slow,
It is so hard to wait.

Over the river, and through the wood—
Old Jowler hears our bells;
He shakes his pow,
With a loud bow wow,
And thus the news he tells.

Over the river, and through the wood—
When grandmother sees us come,
She will say, Oh dear,

The children are here,
Bring a pie for every one.

Over the river, and through the wood—
Now grandmother's cap I spy!
Hurra for the fun!
Is the pudding done?
Hurra for the pumpkin pie!

—*Lydia Maria Child*

Concord Hymn

By the rude bridge that arched the flood,
　　Their flag to April's breeze unfurled,
Here once the embattled farmers stood
　　And fired the shot heard round the world.

The foe long since in silence slept;
　　Alike the conqueror silent sleeps;
And Time the ruined bridge has swept
　　Down the dark stream which seaward creeps.

On the green bank, by this soft stream,
　　We set to-day a votive stone;
That memory may their deed redeem,
　　When, like our sires, our sons are gone.

Spirit, that made those heroes dare
　　To die, and leave their children free,
Bid Time and Nature gently spare
　　The shaft we raise to them and thee.

—Ralph Waldo Emerson

Boston Hymn

The word of the Lord by night
To the watching Pilgrims came,
As they sat by the seaside,
And filled their hearts with flame.

God said, I am tired of kings,
I suffer them no more;
Up to my ear the morning brings
The outrage of the poor.

Think ye I made this ball
A field of havoc and war,
Where tyrants great and tyrants small
Might harry the weak and poor?

My angel,—his name is Freedom,—
Choose him to be your king;
He shall cut pathways east and west
And fend you with his wing.

Lo! I uncover the land
Which I hid of old time in the West,
As the sculptor uncovers the statue
When he has wrought his best;

I show Columbia, of the rocks
Which dip their foot in the seas,

And soar to the air-borne flocks
Of clouds, and the boreal fleece.

I will divide my goods;
Call in the wretch and slave:
None shall rule but the humble,
And none but Toil shall have.

I will have never a noble,
No lineage counted great;
Fishers and choppers and ploughmen
Shall constitute a state.

Go, cut down the trees in the forest
And trim the straightest boughs;
Cut down the trees in the forest
And build me a wooden house.

Call the people together,
The young men and the sires,
The digger in the harvest field,
Hireling, and him that hires;

And here in a pine state-house
They shall choose men to rule
In every needful faculty,
In church, and state, and school.

Lo, now! if these poor men
Can govern the land and sea,
And make just laws below the sun,
As planets faithful be.

And ye shall succor men;
'T is nobleness to serve;
Help them who cannot help again:
Beware from right to swerve.

I break your bonds and masterships,
And I unchain the slave:
Free be his heart and hand henceforth
As wind and wandering wave.

I cause from every creature
His proper good to flow:
As much as he is and doeth,
So much he shall bestow.

But, laying hands on another
To coin his labor and sweat,
He goes in pawn to be his victim
For eternal years in debt.

To-day unbind the captive,
So only are ye unbound;
Lift up a people from the dust,
Trump of their rescue, sound!

Pay ransom to the owner
And fill the bag to the brim.
Who is the owner? The slave is owner,
And ever was. Pay him.

O North! give him beauty for rags,
And honor, O South! for his shame;
Nevada! coin thy golden crags
With Freedom's image and name.

Up! and the dusky race
That sat in darkness long,—
Be swift their feet as antelopes,
And as behemoth strong.

Come, East and West and North,
By races, as snow-flakes,

And carry my purpose forth,
Which neither halts nor shakes.

My will fulfilled shall be,
For, in daylight or in dark,
My thunderbolt has eyes to see
His way home to the mark.

—*Ralph Waldo Emerson*

Paul Revere's Ride

Listen, my children, and you shall hear
Of the midnight ride of Paul Revere,
On the eighteenth of April, in Seventy-five;
Hardly a man is now alive
Who remembers that famous day and year.

He said to his friend, "If the British march
By land or sea from the town to night,
Hang a lantern aloft in the belfry arch
Of the North Church tower as a signal light,—
One, if by land, and two, if by sea;
And I on the opposite shore will be,
Ready to ride and spread the alarm
Through every Middlesex village and farm,
For the country folk to be up and to arm."

Then he said, "Good night!" and with muffled oar
Silently rowed to the Charlestown shore,
Just as the moon rose over the bay,
Where swinging wide at her moorings lay
The Somerset, British man-of-war;
A phantom ship, with each mast and spar
Across the moon like a prison bar,
And a huge black hulk, that was magnified
By its own reflection in the tide.

Meanwhile, his friend, through alley and street,
Wanders and watches with eager ears,
Till in the silence around him he hears
The muster of men at the barrack door,
The sound of arms, and the tramp of feet,
And the measured tread of the grenadiers,
Marching down to their boats on the shore.

Then he climbed the tower of the Old North Church,
By the wooden stairs, with stealthy tread,
To the belfry-chamber overhead,
And startled the pigeons from their perch
On the sombre rafters, that round him made
Masses and moving shapes of shade,—
By the trembling ladder, steep and tall
To the highest window in the wall,
Where he paused to listen and look down
A moment on the roofs of the town,
And the moonlight flowing over all.

Beneath, in the churchyard, lay the dead,
In their night-encampment on the hill,
Wrapped in silence so deep and still
That he could hear, like a sentinel's tread,
The watchful night-wind, as it went
Creeping along from tent to tent,
And seeming to whisper, "All is well!"
A moment only he feels the spell
Of the place and the hour, and the secret dread
Of the lonely belfry and the dead;
For suddenly all his thoughts are bent
On a shadowy something far away,
Where the river widens to meet the bay,—
A line of black that bends and floats
On the rising tide, like a bridge of boats.

Meanwhile, impatient to mount and ride,
Booted and spurred, with a heavy stride
On the opposite shore walked Paul Revere.
Now he patted his horse's side,
Now gazed at the landscape far and near,
Then, impetuous, stamped the earth,
And turned and tightened his saddle-girth;
But mostly he watched with eager search
The belfry-tower of the Old North Church,
As it rose above the graves on the hill,
Lonely and spectral and sombre and still.
And lo! as he looks, on the belfry's height
A glimmer, and then a gleam of light!
He springs to the saddle, the bridle he turns,
But lingers and gazes, till full on his sight
A second lamp in the belfry burns!

A hurry of hoofs in a village street,
A shape in the moonlight, a bulk in the dark,
And beneath, from the pebbles, in passing, a spark
Struck out by a steed flying fearless and fleet:
That was all! And yet, through the gloom and the light,
The fate of a nation was riding that night;
And the spark struck out by that steed, in his flight,
Kindled the land into flame with its heat.

He has left the village and mounted the steep,
And beneath him, tranquil and broad and deep,
Is the Mystic, meeting the ocean tides;
And under the alders that skirt its edge,
Now soft on the sand, now loud on the ledge,
Is heard the tramp of his steed as he rides.

It was twelve by the village clock,
When he crossed the bridge into Medford town.
He heard the crowing of the cock,
And the barking of the farmer's dog,

And felt the damp of the river fog,
That rises after the sun goes down.

It was one by the village clock,
When he galloped into Lexington.
He saw the gilded weathercock
Swim in the moonlight as he passed,
And the meeting-house windows, blank and bare,
Gaze at him with a spectral glare,
As if they already stood aghast
At the bloody work they would look upon.

It was two by the village clock,
When he came to the bridge in Concord town.
He heard the bleating of the flock,
And the twitter of birds among the trees,
And felt the breath of the morning breeze
Blowing over the meadows brown.
And one was safe and asleep in his bed
Who at the bridge would be first to fall,
Who that day would be lying dead,
Pierced by a British musket-ball.

You know the rest. In the books you have read,
How the British Regulars fired and fled,—
How the farmers gave them ball for ball,
From behind each fence and farm-yard wall,
Chasing the red-coats down the lane,
Then crossing the fields to emerge again
Under the trees at the turn of the road,
And only pausing to fire and load.

So through the night rode Paul Revere;
And so through the night went his cry of alarm
To every Middlesex village and farm,—
A cry of defiance and not of fear,
A voice in the darkness, a knock at the door,
And a word that shall echo forevermore!

For, borne on the night-wind of the Past,
Through all our history, to the last,
In the hour of darkness and peril and need,
The people will waken and listen to hear
The hurrying hoof-beats of that steed,
And the midnight message of Paul Revere.

—*Henry Wadsworth Longfellow*

Barbara Frietchie

Up from the meadows rich with corn,
Clear in the cool September morn,

The clustered spires of Frederick stand
Green-walled by the hills of Maryland.

Round about them orchards sweep,
Apple and peach tree fruited deep,

Fair as the garden of the Lord
To the eyes of the famished rebel horde,

On that pleasant morn of the early fall
When Lee marched over the mountain-wall;

Over the mountains winding down,
Horse and foot, into Frederick town.

Forty flags with their silver stars,
Forty flags with their crimson bars,

Flapped in the morning wind: the sun
Of noon looked down, and saw not one.

Up rose old Barbara Frietchie then,
Bowed with her fourscore years and ten;

Bravest of all in Frederick town,
She took up the flag the men hauled down;

In her attic window the staff she set,
To show that one heart was loyal yet.

Up the street came the rebel tread,
Stonewall Jackson riding ahead.

Under his slouched hat left and right
He glanced; the old flag met his sight.

"Halt!"—the dust-brown ranks stood fast.
"Fire!"—out blazed the rifle-blast.

It shivered the window, pane and sash;
It rent the banner with seam and gash.

Quick, as it fell, from the broken staff
Dame Barbara snatched the silken scarf.

She leaned far out on the window-sill,
And shook it forth with a royal will.

"Shoot, if you must, this old gray head,
But spare your country's flag," she said.

A shade of sadness, a blush of shame,
Over the face of the leader came;

The nobler nature within him stirred
To life at that woman's deed and word;

"Who touches a hair of yon gray head
Dies like a dog! March on!" he said.

All day long through Frederick street
Sounded the tread of marching feet:

All day long that free flag tossed
Over the heads of the rebel host.

Ever its torn folds rose and fell
On the loyal winds that loved it well;

And through the hill-gaps sunset light
Shone over it with a warm good-night.

Barbara Frietchie's work is o'er,
And the Rebel rides on his raids no more.

Honor to her! and let a tear
Fall, for her sake, on Stonewall's bier.

Over Barbara Frietchie's grave,
Flag of Freedom and Union, wave!

Peace and order and beauty draw
Round thy symbol of light and law;

And ever the stars above look down
On thy stars below in Frederick town!

—*John Greenleaf Whittier*

America

My country, 'tis of thee,
Sweet land of liberty,
Of thee I sing;
Land where my fathers died,
Land of the Pilgrim's pride,
From ev'ry mountainside
Let freedom ring!

My native country, thee,
Land of the noble free,
Thy name I love;
I love thy rocks and rills,
Thy woods and templed hills;
My heart with rapture thrills,
Like that above.

Let music swell the breeze,
And ring from all the trees
Sweet freedom's song.
Let mortal tongues awake;
Let all that breathe partake;
Let rocks their silence break,
The sound prolong.

Our father's God, to Thee,
Author of liberty,
To Thee we sing.
Long may our land be bright

With freedom's holy light;
Protect us by Thy might,
Great God, our King!

—*Samuel Francis Smith*

Old Ironsides

Ay, tear her tattered ensign down!
  Long has it waved on high,
And many an eye has danced to see
  That banner in the sky;
Beneath it rung the battle shout,
  And burst the cannon's roar;—
The meteor of the ocean air
  Shall sweep the clouds no more.

Her deck, once red with heroes' blood,
  Where knelt the vanquished foe,
When winds were hurrying o'er the flood,
  And waves were white below,
No more shall feel the victor's tread,
  Or know the conquered knee;—
The harpies of the shore shall pluck
  The eagle of the sea!

Oh, better that her shattered hulk
  Should sink beneath the wave;
Her thunders shook the mighty deep,
  And there should be her grave;
Nail to the mast her holy flag,
  Set every threadbare sail,
And give her to the god of storms,
  The lightning and the gale!

—*Oliver Wendell Holmes*

The First Atlantic Telegraph

With outward signs, as well as inward life,
The world is hastening onward to its end!
With higher purposes our Age is rife,
Than those to which with grovelling minds we tend.
For lo! beneath the Atlantic's stormy breast
Is laid, from shore to shore, the Electric Wire;
And words, with speed of thought, from east to west
Dart to and fro on wings that never tire.
May never man, to higher objects blind,
Forget by whom this miracle was wrought;
But worship and adore the Eternal Mind,
Which gave at length to man the wondrous thought;
And on wise-hearted men bestowed the skill
His Providential Purpose to fulfill.

—*Jones Very*

Our Country

It is a noble country where we dwell,
Fit for a stalwart race to summer in;
From Madawaska to Red River raft,
From Florid keys to the Missouri forks,
See what unwearied (and) copious streams
Come tumbling to the east and southern shore,
To find a man stand on their lowland banks:
Behold the innumerous rivers and the licks
Where he may drink to quench his summer's thirst,
And the broad corn and rice fields yonder, where
His hands may gather for his winter's store.

See the fair reaches of the northern lakes
To cool his summer with their inland breeze,
And the long slumbering Appalachian range
Offering its slopes to his unwearied knees!
See what a long-lipped sea doth clip the shores,
And noble strands where navies may find port;
See Boston, Baltimore, and New York stand
Fair in the sunshine on the eastern sea,
And yonder too the fair green prairie.

See the red race with the sullen step retreat,
Emptying its graves, striking the wigwam tent,
And where the rude camps of its brethren stand,
Dotting the distant green, their herds around;
In serried ranks, and with a distant clang,
Their fowl fly o'er, bound to the northern lakes,

Whose plashing waves invite their webbéd feet.
Such the fair reach and prospect of the land,
The journeying summer creeps from south to north
With wearied feet, resting in many a vale;
Its length doth tire the seasons to o'ercome,
Its widening breadth doth make the sea-breeze pause
And spend its breath against the mountain's side:
Still serene Summer paints the southern fields,
While the stern Winter reigns on northern hills.

Look nearer,—know the lineaments of each face,—
Learn the far-travelled race, and find here met
The so long gathering congress of the world!
The Afric race brought here to curse its fate,
Erin to bless,—the patient German too,
Th' industrious Swiss, the fickle, sanguine Gaul,
And manly Saxon, leading all the rest.
All things invite this earth's inhabitants
To rear their lives to an unheard-of height,
And meet the expectation of the land;
To give at length the restless race of man
A pause in the long westering caravan.

—*Henry David Thoreau*

An Ode for the Fourth of July, 1876

Her children shall rise up to bless her name,
And wish her harmless length of days,
The mighty mother of a mighty brood,
Blessed in all tongues and dear to every blood,
The beautiful, the strong, and, best of all, the good.

—*James Russell Lowell*

The Battle Hymn of the Republic

Mine eyes have seen the glory of the coming of the Lord:
He is trampling out the vintage where the grapes of wrath are stored;
He hath loosed the fatal lightning of His terrible swift sword:
    His truth is marching on.

I have seen Him in the watch-fires of a hundred circling camps,
They have builded Him an altar in the evening dews and damps;
I can read His righteous sentence by the dim and flaring lamps:
    His day is marching on.

I have read a fiery gospel writ in burnished rows of steel:
"As ye deal with my contemners, so with you my grace shall deal;
Let the Hero, born of woman, crush the serpent with his heel,
    Since God is marching on."

He has sounded forth the trumpet that shall never call retreat;
He is sifting out the hearts of men before His judgement seat:
Oh, be swift, my soul, to answer Him! Be jubilant, my feet!
    Our God is marching on.

In the beauty of the lilies Christ was born across the sea,
With a glory in his bosom that transfigures you and me:
As he died to make men holy, let us die to make men free,
    While God is marching on.

—*Julia Ward Howe*

Crossing Brooklyn Ferry

1

Flood-tide below me! I see you face to face!
Clouds of the west—sun there half an hour high—I see you
    also face to face.

Crowds of men and women attired in the usual costumes,
    how curious you are to me!
On the ferry-boats the hundreds and hundreds that cross,
    returning home, are more curious to me than you suppose,
And you that shall cross from shore to shore years hence
    are more to me, and more in my meditations, than you
    might suppose.

The impalpable sustenance of me from all things at all hours of the day,
The simple, compact, well-join'd scheme, myself disintegrated,
    every one disintegrated yet part of the scheme,
The similitudes of the past and those of the future,
The glories strung like beads on my smallest sights and hearings,
    on the walk in the street and the passage over the river,
The current rushing so swiftly and swimming with me far away,
The others that are to follow me, the ties between me and them,
The certainty of others, the life, love, sight, hearing of others.

Others will enter the gates of the ferry and cross from shore to shore,
Others will watch the run of the flood-tide,
Others will see the shipping of Manhattan north and west,
    and the heights of Brooklyn to the south and east,
Others will see the islands large and small;
Fifty years hence, others will see them as they cross,
    the sun half an hour high,
A hundred years hence, or ever so many hundred years hence,
    others will see them,
Will enjoy the sunset, the pouring-in of the flood-tide,
    the falling-back to the sea of the ebb-tide.

3

It avails not, time nor place—distance avails not,
I am with you, you men and women of a generation,
    or ever so many generations hence,
Just as you feel when you look on the river and sky, so I felt,
Just as any of you is one of a living crowd, I was one of a crowd,
Just as you are refresh'd by the gladness of the river and the bright flow,
    I was refresh'd,
Just as you stand and lean on the rail, yet hurry with the swift current,
    I stood yet was hurried,
Just as you look on the numberless masts of ships and the thick-stemm'd
    pipes of steamboats, I look'd.

I too many and many a time cross'd the river of old,
Watched the Twelfth-month sea-gulls, saw them high in the air floating
    with motionless wings, oscillating their bodies,
Saw how the glistening yellow lit up parts of their bodies and left the rest
    in strong shadow,
Saw the slow-wheeling circles and the gradual edging toward the south,
Saw the reflection of the summer sky in the water,
Had my eyes dazzled by the shimmering track of beams,
Look'd at the fine centrifugal spokes of light round the shape of my
    head in the sunlit water,
Look'd on the haze on the hills southward and south-westward,

Look'd on the vapor as it flew in fleeces tinged with violet,
Look'd toward the lower bay to notice the vessels arriving,
Saw their approach, saw aboard those that were near me,
Saw the white sails of schooners and sloops, saw the ships at anchor,
The sailors at work in the rigging or out astride the spars,
The round masts, the swinging motion of the hulls,
    the slender serpentine pennants,
The large and small steamers in motion, the pilots in their pilot-houses,
The white wake left by the passage, the quick tremulous whirl
    of the wheels,
The flags of all nations, the falling of them at sunset,
The scallop-edged waves in the twilight, the ladled cups,
    the frolicsome crests and glistening,
The stretch afar growing dimmer and dimmer, the gray walls
    of the granite storehouses by the docks,
On the river the shadowy group, the big steam-tug closely flank'd
    on each side by the barges, the hay-boat, the belated lighter,
On the neighboring shore the fires from the foundry chimneys burning
    high and glaringly into the night,
Casting their flicker of black contrasted with wild red and yellow light
    over the tops of houses, and down into the clefts of streets.

4

These and all else were to me the same as they are to you,
I loved well those cities, loved well the stately and rapid river,
The men and women I saw were all near to me,
Others the same—others who look back on me because I look'd forward
    to them,
(The time will come, though I stop here to-day and to-night.)

5

What is it then between us?
What is the count of the scores or hundreds of years between us?

Whatever it is, it avails not—distance avails not, and place avails not,
I too lived, Brooklyn of ample hills was mine,
I too walk'd the streets of Manhattan island, and bathed
    in the waters around it,
I too felt the curious abrupt questionings stir within me,
In the day among crowds of people sometimes they came upon me,
In my walks home late at night or as I lay in my bed
    they came upon me,
I too had been struck from the float forever held in solution,
I too had receiv'd identity by my body,
That I was I knew was of my body, and what I should be I knew
    I should be of my body.

6

It is not upon you alone the dark patches fall,
The dark threw its patches down upon me also,
The best I had done seem'd to me blank and suspicious,
My great thoughts as I supposed them, were they not in reality meagre?
Nor is it you alone who know what it is to be evil,
I am he who knew what it was to be evil,
I too knitted the old knot of contrariety,
Blabb'd, blush'd, resented, lied, stole, grudg'd,
Had guile, anger, lust, hot wishes I dared not speak,
Was wayward, vain, greedy, shallow, sly, cowardly, malignant,
The wolf, the snake, the hog, not wanting in me,
The cheating look, the frivolous word, the adulterous wish, not wanting,
Refusals, hates, postponements, meanness, laziness, none
    of these wanting,
Was one with the rest, the days and haps of the rest,
Was call'd by my nighest name by clear loud voices of young men
    as they saw me approaching or passing,
Felt their arms on my neck as I stood, or the negligent leaning
    of their flesh against me as I sat,
Saw many I loved in the street or ferry-boat or public assembly,
    yet never told them a word,

Lived the same life with the rest, the same old laughing,
    gnawing, sleeping,
Play'd the part that still looks back on the actor or actress,
The same old role, the role that is what we make it, as great as we like,
Or as small as we like, or both great and small.

7

Closer yet I approach you,
What thought you have of me now, I had as much of you—
    I laid in my stores in advance,
I consider'd long and seriously of you before you were born.

Who was to know what should come home to me?
Who knows but I am enjoying this?
Who knows, for all the distance, but I am as good as looking
    at you now, for all you cannot see me?

8

Ah, what can ever be more stately and admirable to me
    than mast-hemm'd Manhattan?
River and sunset and scallop-edg'd waves of flood-tide?
The sea-gulls oscillating their bodies, the hay-boat
    in the twilight, and the belated lighter?
What gods can exceed these that clasp me by the hand, and with voices
    I love call me promptly and loudly by my nighest name
    as I approach?
What is more subtle than this which ties me to the woman
    or man that looks in my face?
Which fuses me into you now, and pours my meaning into you?

We understand then do we not?
What I promis'd without mentioning it, have you not accepted?
What the study could not teach—what the preaching
    could not accomplish is accomplish'd, is it not?

Flow on, river! flow with the flood-tide, and ebb with the ebb-tide!
Frolic on, crested and scallop-edg'd waves!
Gorgeous clouds of the sunset! drench with your splendor me,
    or the men and women generations after me!
Cross from shore to shore, countless crowds of passengers!
Stand up, tall masts of Mannahatta! stand up, beautiful hills of Brooklyn!
Throb, baffled and curious brain! throw out questions and answers!
Suspend here and everywhere, eternal float of solution!
Gaze, loving and thirsting eyes, in the house or street or public assembly!
Sound out, voices of young men! loudly and musically call me
    by my nighest name!
Live, old life! play the part that looks back on the actor or actress!
Play the old role, the role that is great or small according as one makes it!
Consider, you who peruse me, whether I may not in unknown ways
    be looking upon you;
Be firm, rail over the river, to support those who lean idly, yet haste
    with the hasting current;
Fly on, sea-birds! fly sideways, or wheel in large circles high in the air;
Receive the summer sky, you water, and faithfully hold it
    till all downcast eyes have time to take it from you!

Diverge, fine spokes of light, from the shape of my head,
    or any one's head, in the sunlit water!
Come on, ships from the lower bay! pass up or down,
    white-sail'd schooners, sloops, lighters!
Flaunt away, flags of all nations! be duly lower'd at sunset!
Burn high your fires, foundry chimneys! cast black shadows at nightfall!
    cast red and yellow light over the tops of the houses!
Appearances, now or henceforth, indicate what you are,
You necessary film, continue to envelop the soul,
About my body for me, and your body for you, be hung
    our divinest aromas,
Thrive, cities—bring your freight, bring your shows, ample
    and sufficient rivers,
Expand, being than which none else is perhaps more spiritual,
Keep your places, objects than which none else is more lasting.

You have waited, you always wait, you dumb, beautiful ministers,
We receive you with free sense at last, and are insatiate henceforward,
Not you any more shall be able to foil us, or withhold yourselves
    from us,
We use you, and do not cast you aside—we plant you permanently
    within us,
We fathom you not—we love you—there is perfection in you also,
You furnish your parts toward eternity,
Great or small, you furnish your parts toward the soul.

—*Walt Whitman*

City of Orgies

City of orgies, walks and joys,
City whom that I have lived and sung in your midst will one day
    make you illustrious,
Not the pageants of you, not your shifting tableaus,
    your spectacles, repay me,
Not the interminable rows of your houses, nor the ships at the wharves,
Nor the processions in the streets, nor the bright windows with goods
    in them,
Nor to converse with learn'd persons, or bear my share in the soiree
    or feast;
Not those, but as I pass O Manhattan, your frequent and swift
    flash of eyes offering me love,
Offering response to my own—these repay me,
Lovers, continual lovers, only repay me.

—*Walt Whitman*

A Promise to California

A promise to California,
Or inland to the great pastoral Plains, and on to Puget sound and
      Oregon;
Sojourning east a while longer, soon I travel toward you, to remain,
      to teach robust American love,
For I know very well that I and robust love belong among you,
      inland, and along the Western sea;
For these States tend inland and toward the Western sea, and I
      will also.

—Walt Whitman

I Hear America Singing

I hear America singing, the varied carols I hear,
Those of mechanics, each one singing his as it should be
    blithe and strong,
The carpenter singing his as he measures his plank or beam,
The mason singing his as he makes ready for work,
    or leaves off work,
The boatman singing what belongs to him in his boat,
    the deckhand singing on the steamboat deck,
The shoemaker singing as he sits on his bench, the hatter singing
    as he stands,
The wood-cutter's song, the ploughboy's on his way in the morning,
    or at noon intermission or at sundown,
The delicious singing of the mother, or of the young wife at work,
    or of the girl sewing or washing,
Each singing what belongs to him or her and to none else,
The day what belongs to the day—at night the party of young fellows,
    robust, friendly,
Singing with open mouths their strong melodious songs.

—*Walt Whitman*

Ball's Bluff

A Reverie (October 1861)

One noonday, at my window in the town,
  I saw a sight—saddest that eyes can see—
  Young soldiers marching lustily
      Unto the wars,
With fifes, and flags in mottoed pageantry;
      While all the porches, walks, and doors
Were rich with ladies cheering royally.

They moved like Juny morning on the wave,
  Their hearts were fresh as clover in its prime
  (It was the breezy summer time),
      Life throbbed so strong,
How should they dream that Death in rosy clime
      Would come to thin their shining throng?
Youth feels immortal, like the gods sublime.

Weeks passed; and at my window, leaving bed,
  By night I mused, of easeful sleep bereft,
  On those brave boys (Ah War! thy theft);
      Some marching feet
Found pause at last by cliffs Potomac cleft;
      Wakeful I mused, while in the street
Far footfalls died away till none were left.

—*Herman Melville*

53

America

America, it is to thee,
Thou boasted land of liberty,—
It is to thee I raise my song,
Thou land of blood, and crime, and wrong.
It is to thee, my native land,
From whence has issued many a band
To tear the black man from his soil,
And force him here to delve and toil;
Chained on your blood-bemoistened sod,
Cringing beneath a tyrant's rod,
Stripped of those rights which Nature's God
   Bequeathed to all the human race,
Bound to a petty tyrant's nod,
   Because he wears a paler face.
Was it for this, that freedom's fires
Were kindled by your patriot sires?
Was it for this, they shed their blood,
On hill and plain, on field and flood?
Was it for this, that wealth and life
Were staked upon that desperate strife,
Which drenched this land for seven long years
With blood of men, and women's tears?
When black and white fought side by side,
   Upon the well-contested field,—
Turned back the fierce opposing tide,
   And made the proud invader yield—
When, wounded, side by side they lay,
   And heard with joy the proud hurrah

From their victorious comrades say
    That they had waged successful war,
The thought ne'er entered in their brains
That they endured those toils and pains,
To forge fresh fetters, heavier chains
For their own children, in whose veins
Should flow that patriotic blood,
So freely shed on field and flood.
Oh no; they fought, as they believed,
    For the inherent rights of man;
But mark, how they have been deceived
    By slavery's accursed plan.
They never thought, when thus they shed
    Their heart's best blood, in freedom's cause,
That their own sons would live in dread,
    Under unjust, oppressive laws:
That those who quietly enjoyed
    The rights for which they fought and fell,
Could be the framers of a code,
    That would disgrace the fiends of hell!
Could they have looked, with prophet's ken,
    Down to the present evil time,
    Seen free-born men, uncharged with crime,
Consigned unto a slaver's pen,—
Or thrust into a prison cell,
With thieves and murderers to dwell—
While that same flag whose stripes and stars
Had been their guide through freedom's wars
As proudly waved above the pen
Of dealers in the souls of men!
Or could the shades of all the dead,
    Who fell beneath that starry flag,
Visit the scenes where they once bled,
    On hill and plain, on vale and crag,
By peaceful brook, or ocean's strand,
    By inland lake, or dark green wood,
Where'er the soil of this wide land
    Was moistened by their patriot blood,—

And then survey the country o'er,
    From north to south, from east to west,
And hear the agonizing cry
Ascending up to God on high,
From western wilds to ocean's shore,
    The fervent prayer of the oppressed;
The cry of helpless infancy
    Torn from the parent's fond caress
By some base tool of tyranny,
    And doomed to woe and wretchedness;
The indignant wail of fiery youth,
    Its noble aspirations crushed,
Its generous zeal, its love of truth,
    Trampled by tyrants in the dust;
The aerial piles which fancy reared,
    And hopes too bright to be enjoyed,
Have passed and left his young heart seared,
    And all its dreams of bliss destroyed.
The shriek of virgin purity,
    Doomed to some libertine's embrace,
Should rouse the strongest sympathy
    Of each one of the human race;
And weak old age, oppressed with care,
    As he reviews the scene of strife,
Puts up to God a fervent prayer,
    To close his dark and troubled life.
The cry of fathers, mothers, wives,
    Severed from all their hearts hold dear,
And doomed to spend their wretched lives
    In gloom, and doubt, and hate, and fear;
And manhood, too, with soul of fire,
And arm of strength, and smothered ire,
Stands pondering with brow of gloom,
Upon his dark unhappy doom,
Whether to plunge in battle's strife,
And buy his freedom with his life,
And with stout heart and weapon strong,
Pay back the tyrant wrong for wrong,

Or wait the promised time of God,
    When his Almighty ire shall wake,
And smite the oppressor in his wrath,
And hurl red ruin in his path,
And with the terrors of his rod,
    Cause adamantine hearts to quake.
Here Christian writhes in bondage still,
    Beneath his brother Christian's rod,
And pastors trample down at will,
    The image of the living God.
While prayers go up in lofty strains,
    And pealing hymns ascend to heaven,
The captive, toiling in his chains,
    With tortured limbs and bosom riven,
Raises his fettered hand on high,
    And in the accents of despair,
To him who rules both earth and sky,
    Puts up a sad, a fervent prayer,
To free him from the awful blast
    Of slavery's bitter galling shame—
Although his portion should be cast
    With demons in eternal flame!
Almighty God! 't is this they call
    The land of liberty and law;
Part of its sons in baser thrall
    Than Babylon or Egypt saw—
Worse scenes of rapine, lust and shame,
    Than Babylonian ever knew,
Are perpetrated in the name
    Of God, the holy, just, and true;
And darker doom than Egypt felt,
May yet repay this nation's guilt.
Almighty God! thy aid impart,
And fire anew each faltering heart,
And strengthen every patriot's hand,
Who aims to save our native land.
We do not come before thy throne,
    With carnal weapons drenched in gore,

Although our blood has freely flown,
    In adding to the tyrant's store.
Father! before thy throne we come,
    Not in the panoply of war,
With pealing trump, and rolling drum,
    And cannon booming loud and far;
Striving in blood to wash out blood,
    Through wrong to seek redress for wrong;
For while thou'rt holy, just and good,
    The battle is not to the strong;
But in the sacred name of peace,
    Of justice, virtue, love and truth,
We pray, and never mean to cease,
    Till weak old age and fiery youth
In freedom's cause their voices raise,
And burst the bonds of every slave;
Till, north and south, and east and west,
The wrongs we bear shall be redressed.

—*James Monroe Whitfield*

The Slave Mother

Heard you that shriek? It rose
   So wildly on the air,
It seemed as if a burden'd heart
   Was breaking in despair.

Saw you those hands so sadly clasped—
   The bowed and feeble head—
The shuddering of that fragile form—
   That look of grief and dread?

Saw you the sad, imploring eye?
   Its every glance was pain,
As if a storm of agony
   Were sweeping through the brain.

She is a mother, pale with fear,
   Her boy clings to her side,
And in her kirtle vainly tries
   His trembling form to hide.

He is not hers, although she bore
   For him a mother's pains;
He is not hers, although her blood
   Is coursing through his veins!

He is not hers, for cruel hands
   May rudely tear apart

The only wreath of household love
    That binds her breaking heart.

His love has been a joyous light
    That o'er her pathway smiled,
A fountain gushing ever new,
    Amid life's desert wild.

His lightest word has been a tone
    Of music round her heart,
Their lives a streamlet blent in one—
    Oh, Father! must they part?

They tear him from her circling arms,
    Her last and fond embrace.
Oh! never more may her sad eyes
    Gaze on his mournful face.

No marvel, then, these bitter shrieks
    Disturb the listening air:
She is a mother, and her heart
    Is breaking in despair.

—Frances E. W. Harper

Learning to Read

Very soon the Yankee teachers
   Came down and set up school;
But, oh! how the Rebs did hate it,—
   It was agin' their rule.

Our masters always tried to hide
   Book learning from our eyes;
Knowledge did'nt agree with slavery—
   'Twould make us all too wise.

But some of us would try to steal
   A little from the book,
And put the words together,
   And learn by hook or crook.

I remember Uncle Caldwell,
   Who took pot-liquor fat
And greased the pages of his book,
   And hid it in his hat.

And had his master ever seen
   The leaves upon his head,
He'd have thought them greasy papers,
   But nothing to be read.

And there was Mr. Turner's Ben,
   Who heard the children spell,

And picked the words right up by heart,
  And learned to read 'em well.

Well, the Northern folks kept sending
  The Yankee teachers down;
And they stood right up and helped us,
  Though Rebs did sneer and frown.

And, I longed to read my Bible,
  For precious words it said;
But when I begun to learn it,
  Folks just shook their heads.

And said there is no use trying,
  Oh! Chloe, you're too late;
But as I was rising sixty,
  I had no time to wait.

So I got a pair of glasses,
  And straight to work I went,
And never stopped till I could read
  The hymns and Testament.

Then I got a little cabin—
  A place to call my own—
And I felt as independent
  As the queen upon her throne.

      —*Frances E. W. Harper*

Ode Sung at Magnolia Cemetery

1.

Sleep sweetly in your humble graves,
　　Sleep, martyrs of a fallen cause;
Though yet no marble column craves
　　The pilgrim here to pause.

2.

In seeds of laurel in the earth
　　The blossom of your fame is blown,
And somewhere, waiting for its birth,
　　The shaft is in the stone!

3.

Meanwhile, behalf the tardy years
　　Which keep in trust your storied tombs,
Behold! your sisters bring their tears,
　　And these memorial blooms.

4.

Small tributes! but your shades will smile
　　More proudly on these wreaths to-day,

Than when some cannon-moulded pile
  Shall overlook this bay.

5.

Stoop, angels, hither from the skies!
  There is no holier spot of ground
Than where defeated valor lies,
  By mourning beauty crowned!

—*Henry Timrod*

#389

There's been a Death, in the Opposite House,
As lately as Today –
I know it, by the numb look
Such Houses have – alway –

The Neighbors rustle in and out –
The Doctor – drives away –
A Window opens like a Pod –
Abrupt – mechanically –

Somebody flings a Mattress out –
The Children hurry by –
They wonder if it died – on that –
I used to – when a Boy –

The Minister – goes stiffly in –
As if the House were His –
And He owned all the Mourners – now –
And little Boys – besides –

And then the Milliner – and the Man
Of the Appalling Trade –
To take the measure of the House –

There'll be that Dark Parade –

Of Tassels – and of Coaches – soon –
It's easy as a Sign –

The Intuition of the News –
In just a Country Town –

—Emily Dickinson

#617

Don't put up my Thread and Needle –
I'll begin to Sew
When the Birds begin to whistle –
Better Stitches – so –

These were bent – my sight got crooked –
When my mind – is plain
I'll do seams – a Queen's endeavor
Would not blush to own –

Hems – too fine for Lady's tracing
To the sightless Knot –
Tucks – of dainty interspersion –
Like a dotted Dot –

Leave my Needle in the furrow –
Where I put it down –
I can make the zigzag stitches
Straight – when I am strong –

Till then – dreaming I am sewing
Fetch the seam I missed –
Closer – so I – at my sleeping –
Still surmise I stitch –

—*Emily Dickinson*

At Home from Church

The lilacs lift in generous bloom
    Their plumes of dear old-fashioned flowers;
Their fragrance fills the still old house
    Where left alone I count the hours.

High in the apple-trees the bees
    Are humming, busy in the sun,—
An idle robin cries for rain
    But once or twice and then is done.

The Sunday-morning quiet holds
    In heavy slumber all the street,
While from the church, just out of sight
    Behind the elms, comes slow and sweet

The organ's drone, the voices faint
    That sing the quaint long-meter hymn—
I somehow feel as if shut out
    From some mysterious temple, dim

And beautiful with blue and red
    And golden lights from windows high,
Where angels in the shadows stand
    And earth seems very near the sky.

The day-dream fades—and so I try
    Again to catch the tune that brings

No thought of temple nor of priest,
But only of voice that sings.

—*Sarah Orne Jewett*

Long Island Sound

I see it as it looked one afternoon
In August, – by a fresh soft breeze o'erblown.
The swiftness of the tide, the light thereon,
A far-off sail, white as a crescent moon.
The shining waters with pale currents strewn,
The quiet fishing-smacks, the Eastern cove,
The semi-circle of its dark, green grove.
The luminous grasses, and the merry sun
In the grave sky; the sparkle far and wide,
Laughter of unseen children, cheerful chirp
Of crickets, and low lisp of rippling tide,
Light summer clouds fantastical as sleep
Changing unnoted while I gazed thereon.
All these fair sounds and sights I made my own.

—Emma Lazarus

The New Colossus

Not like the brazen giant of Greek fame,
With conquering limbs astride from land to land;
Here at our sea-washed, sunset gates shall stand
A mighty woman with a torch, whose flame
Is the imprisoned lightning, and her name
Mother of Exiles. From her beacon-hand
Glows world-wide welcome; her mild eyes command
The air-bridged harbor that twin cities frame.
"Keep, ancient lands, your storied pomp!" cries she
With silent lips. "Give me your tired, your poor,
Your huddled masses yearning to breathe free,
The wretched refuse of your teeming shore.
Send these, the homeless, tempest-tossed to me,
I lift my lamp beside the golden door!"

—*Emma Lazarus*

Excerpt, The Old Swimmin'-Hole

Oh! the old swimmin'-hole! whare the crick so still and deep
Looked like a baby-river that was laying half asleep,
And the gurgle of the worter round the drift jest below
Sounded like the laugh of something we onc't ust to know
Before we could remember anything but the eyes
Of the angels lookin' out as we left Paradise;
But the merry days of youth is beyond our controle,
And it's hard to part ferever with the old swimmin'-hole.

Oh! the old swimmin'-hole! In the happy days of yore,
When I ust to lean above it on the old sickamore,
Oh! it showed me a face in its warm sunny tide
That gazed back at me so gay and glorified,
It made me love myself, as I leaped to caress
My shadder smilin' up at me with sich tenderness.
But them days is past and gone, and old Time's tuck his toll
From the old man come back to the old swimmin'-hole.

Oh! the old swimmin'-hole! In the long, lazy days
When the humdrum of school made so many run-a-ways,
How plesant was the jurney down the old dusty lane,
Whare the tracks of our bare feet was all printed so plane
You could tell by the dent of the heel and the sole
They was lots o' fun on hands at the old swimmin'-hole.
But the lost joys is past! Let your tears in sorrow roll
Like the rain that ust to dapple up the old swimmin'-hole.

—*James Whitcomb Riley*

The Anti-Suffragists

Fashionable women in luxurious homes,
With men to feed them, clothe them, pay their bills,
Bow, doff the hat, and fetch the handkerchief;
Hostess or guest, and always so supplied
With graceful deference and courtesy;
Surrounded by their servants, horses, dogs,—
These tell us they have all the rights they want.

Successful women who have won their way
Alone, with strength of their unaided arm,
Or helped by friends, or softly climbing up
By the sweet aid of 'woman's influence';
Successful any way, and caring naught
For any other woman's unsuccess,—
These tell us they have all the rights they want.

Religious women of the feebler sort,—
Not the religion of a righteous world,
A free, enlightened, upward-reaching world,
But the religion that considers life
As something to back out of! – whose ideal
Is to renounce, submit, and sacrifice,
Counting on being patted on the head
And given a high chair when they get to heaven,—
These tell us they have all the rights they want.

Ignorant woman – college-bred sometimes,
But ignorant of life's realities
And principles of righteous government,
And how the privileges they enjoy
Were won with blood and tears by those before—
Those they condemn, whose ways they now oppose;
Saying, 'Why not let well enough alone?
Our world is very pleasant as it is,'—
These tell us they have all the rights they want.

And selfish women, – pigs in petticoats,—
Rich, poor, wise, unwise, top or bottom round,
But all sublimely innocent of thought,
And guiltless of ambition, save the one
Deep, voiceless aspiration – to be fed!
These have no use for rights or duties more.
Duties today are more than they can meet,
And law insures their right to clothes and food,—
These tell us they have all the rights they want.

And, more's the pity, some good women, too;
Good conscientious women, with ideas;
Who think – or think they think – that woman's cause
Is best advanced by letting it alone;
That she somehow is not a human thing,
And not to be helped on by human means,
Just added to humanity – an 'L'—
A wing, a branch, an extra, not mankind,—
These tell us they have all the rights they want.

And out of these has come a monstrous thing,
A strange, down-sucking whirlpool of disgrace,
Women uniting against womanhood,
And using that great name to hide their sin!
Vain are their words as that old king's command
Who set his will against the rising tide.
But who shall measure the historic shame

Of these poor traitors – traitors are they all—
To great Democracy and Womanhood!

—*Charlotte Perkins Gilman*

Cabins

They was dirt-roofed, an' homely, an' ramblin', an' squat—
Jest logs with mud-daubin'; but I loved 'em a lot.
Their latch-strings was out, an' their doors wouldn't lock:
Get down an' walk in ('twas politer to knock).
Mebby nobody home, but the grub was still there;
He'p yerse'f, leave a note, to show you was square;
Might be gone for a week; stay as long as you please,
You knowed you was welcome as a cool summer breeze;
Might be spring 'fore you'd see him, then he'd grin an' declare
He'd a-give a good hoss if he' only been there.
But he's gone with a smile, an' the dear little shack
With his brand on its door won't never come back.
An' his latch-strings is hid with the spirit an' ways
That gladdened our hearts in them good early days.
There wasn't a fence in the world that we knew,
For the West an' its people was honest an' new,
And the range spread away with the sky for a lid—
I'm old, but I'm glad that I lived when I did.

—*Frank Bird Linderman*

War Is Kind

Do not weep, maiden, for war is kind.
Because your lover threw wild hands toward the sky
And the affrighted steed ran on alone,
Do not weep.
War is kind.

> Hoarse, booming drums of the regiment,
> Little souls who thirst for fight,
> These men were born to drill and die.
> The unexplained glory flies above them,
> Great is the battle-god, great, and his kingdom—
> A field where a thousand corpses lie.

Do not weep, babe, for war is kind.
Because your father tumbled in the yellow trenches,
Raged at his breast, gulped and died,
Do not weep.
War is kind.

> Swift blazing flag of the regiment,
> Eagle with crest of red and gold,
> These men were born to drill and die.
> Point for them the virtue of slaughter,
> Make plain to them the excellence of killing
> And a field where a thousand corpses lie.

Mother whose heart hung humble as a button
On the bright splendid shroud of your son,
Do not weep.
War is kind.

—*Stephen Crane*

Thompson's Lunch Room—
Grand Central Station

Study in Whites

Wax-white—
Floor, ceiling, walls.
Ivory shadows
Over the pavement
Polished to cream surfaces
By constant sweeping.
The big room is coloured like the petals
Of a great magnolia,
And has a patina
Of flower bloom
Which makes it shine dimly
Under the electric lamps.
Chairs are ranged in rows
Like sepia seeds
Waiting fulfilment.
The chalk-white spot of a cook's cap
Moves unglossily against the vaguely bright wall—
Dull chalk-white striking the retina like a blow
Through the wavering uncertainty of steam.
Vitreous-white of glasses with green reflections.
Ice-green carboys, shifting—greener, bluer—with the jar of
    moving water.
Jagged green-white bowls of pressed glass
Rearing snow-peaks of chipped sugar

Above the lighthouse-shaped castors
Of grey pepper and grey-white salt.
Grey-white placards: "Oyster Stew, Cornbeef Hash, Frankfurters":
Marble slabs veined with words in meandering lines.
Dropping on the white counter like horn notes
Through a web of violins,
The flat yellow lights of oranges,
The cube-red splashes of apples,
In high plated *épergnes*.
The electric clock jerks every half-minute:
"Coming!—Past!"
"Three beef-steaks and a chicken-pie,"
Bawled through a slide while the clock jerks heavily.
A man carries a china mug of coffee to a distant chair.
Two rice puddings and a salmon salad
Are pushed over the counter;
The unfulfilled chairs open to receive them.
A spoon falls upon the floor with the impact of metal striking stone,
And the sound throws across the room
Sharp, invisible zigzags
Of silver.

—*Amy Lowell*

The Dude Ranch

We used to run a cow-ranch,
In all that old term meant,
But all our ancient glories
In recent years have went;
We're takin' summer boarders,
And, puttin' it quite rude,
It's now the cowboy's province
To herd the festive dude.
We used to run an outfit,
The greatest in the West;
Our cowboys were the wonders—
Our roundups were the best;
The punchers still are with us,
But now they merely guide
The tenderfoot from Boston
Who's learnin' how to ride.
We used to brand our cattle
And ship 'em wide and far;
But now we import humans
From off the Pullman car;
The dudes have got us captures
And tied and branded, too;
And the cowboy's readin' Ibsen
When his daily toil is through.

—Arthur Chapman

After Apple-Picking

My long two-pointed ladder's sticking through a tree
Toward heaven still,
And there's a barrel that I didn't fill
Beside it, and there may be two or three
Apples I didn't pick upon some bough.
But I am done with apple-picking now.
Essence of winter sleep is on the night,
The scent of apples: I am drowsing off.
I cannot rub the strangeness from my sight
I got from looking through a pane of glass
I skimmed this morning from the drinking trough
And held against the world of hoary grass.
It melted, and I let it fall and break.
But I was well
Upon my way to sleep before it fell,
And I could tell
What form my dreaming was about to take.
Magnified apples appear and disappear,
Stem end and blossom end,
And every fleck of russet showing clear.
My instep arch not only keeps the ache,
It keeps the pressure of a ladder-round.
I feel the ladder sway as the boughs bend.
And I keep hearing from the cellar bin
The rumbling sound
Of load on load of apples coming in.
For I have had too much
Of apple-picking: I am overtired

Of the great harvest I myself desired.
There were ten thousand thousand fruit to touch,
Cherish in hand, lift down, and not let fall.
For all
That struck the earth,
No matter if not bruised or spiked with stubble,
Went surely to the cider-apple heap
As of no worth.
One can see what will trouble
This sleep of mine, whatever sleep it is.
Were he not gone,
The woodchuck could say whether it's like his
Long sleep, as I describe its coming on,
Or just some human sleep.

—*Robert Frost*

I Sit and Sew

I sit and sew—a useless task it seems,
My hands grown tired, my head weighed down with dreams—
The panoply of war, the martial tred of men,
Grim-faced, stern-eyed, gazing beyond the ken
Of lesser souls, whose eyes have not seen Death,
Nor learned to hold their lives but as a breath—
But—I must sit and sew.

I sit and sew—my heart aches with desire—
That pageant terrible, that fiercely pouring fire
On wasted fields, and writhing grotesque things
Once men. My soul in pity flings
Appealing cries, yearning only to go
There in that holocaust of hell, those fields of woe—
But—I must sit and sew.

The little useless seam, the idle patch;
Why dream I here beneath my homely thatch,
When there they lie in sodden mud and rain,
Pitifully calling me, the quick ones and the slain?
You need me, Christ! It is no roseate dream
That beckons me—this pretty futile seam,
It stifles me—God, must I sit and sew?

—*Alice Moore Dunbar Nelson*

Work Gangs

Box cars run by a mile long.
And I wonder what they say to each other
When they stop a mile long on a sidetrack.
        Maybe their chatter goes:
I came from Fargo with a load of wheat up to the danger line.
I came from Omaha with a load of shorthorns and they splintered
    my boards.
I came from Detroit heavy with a load of flivvers.
I carried apples from the Hood River last year and this year bunches
    of bananas from Florida; they look for me with watermelons from
    Mississippi next year.

Hammers and shovels of work gangs sleep in shop corners
when the dark stars come on the sky and the night watchmen walk
    and look.

Then the hammer heads talk to the handles,
then the scoops of the shovels talk,
how the day's work nicked and trimmed them,
how they swung and lifted all day,
how the hands of the work gangs smelled of hope.
In the night of the dark stars
when the curve of the sky is a work gang handle,
in the night on the mile long sidetracks,
in the night where the hammers and shovels sleep in corners,
the night watchmen stuff their pipes with dreams—
and sometimes they doze and don't care for nothin',

and sometimes they search their heads for meanings, stories, stars.
   The stuff of it runs like this:
A long way we come; a long way to go; long rests and long deep sniffs
   for our lungs on the way.
Sleep is a belonging of all; even if all songs are old songs and the
   singing heart is snuffed out like a switchman's lantern with the oil
   gone, even if we forget our names and houses in the finish, the
   secret of sleep is left us, sleep belongs to all, sleep is the first and
   last and best of all.

People singing; people with song mouths connecting with song hearts;
   people who must sing or die; people whose song hearts break if
   there is no song mouth; these are my people.

                                        —*Carl Sandburg*

The Flower-Fed Buffaloes

The flower-fed buffaloes of the spring
In the days of long ago,
Ranged where the locomotives sing
And the prarie flowers lie low:—
The tossing, blooming, perfumed grass
Is swept away by wheat,
Wheels and wheels and wheels spin by
In the spring that still is sweet.
But the flower-fed buffaloes of the spring
Left us, long ago.
They gore no more, they bellow no more:—
With the Blackfeet lying low,
With the Pawnee lying low,
Lying low.

—*Vachel Lindsay*

Fabliau of Florida

Baroque of phosphor
On the palmy beach,

Move outward into heaven,
Into the alabasters
And night blues.

Foam and cloud are one.
Sultry moon-monsters
Are dissolving.

Fill your black hull
With white moonlight.

There will never be an end
To this droning of the surf.

—*Wallace Stevens*

Anecdote of the Jar

I placed a jar in Tennessee,
And round it was, upon a hill.
It made the slovenly wilderness
Surround that hill.

The wilderness rose up to it,
And sprawled around, no longer wild.
The jar was round upon the ground
And tall and of a port in air.

It took dominion everywhere.
The jar was gray and bare.
It did not give of bird or bush,
Like nothing else in Tennessee.

—*Wallace Stevens*

The Legend
of Boastful Bill

At a round-up on the Gily
One sweet mornin' long ago,
Ten of us was throwed quite freely
By a hawse from Idaho.
An' we thought he'd go a-beggin'
For a man to break his pride
Till, a-hitchin' up one leggin',
Boastful Bill cut loose an' cried:
"I'm a ornery proposition for to hurt,
I fulfill my earthly mission with a quirt,
I can ride the highest liver
'Tween the Gulf an' Powder River,
And I'll break this thing as easy as I'd flirt."
So Bill climbed the Northern Fury
And they mangled up the air
Till a native of Missouri
Would have owned his brag was fair.
Though the plunges kept him reelin'
And the wind it flapped his shirt,
Loud above the hawse's squealin'
We could hear our friend assert:
"I'm the one to take such rakin's as a joke;
Someone hand me up the makin's of a smoke!
If you think my fame needs brightnin',
Why, I'll rope a streak o' lightnin'
And I'll cinch 'im up and spur 'im till he's broke."

Then one caper of repulsion
Broke that hawse's back in two,
Cinches snapped in the convulsion,
Skyward man and saddle flew,
Up they mounted, never flaggin',
And we watched them through our tears,
While this last, thin bit o'braggin'
Came a-floatin' to our ears:
"If you ever watched my habits very close,
You would know I broke such rabbits by the gross.
I have kept my talent hidin',
I'm too good for earthly ridin',
So I'm off to bust the lightnin'—Adios!"
Years have passed since the ascension;
Boastful Bill ain't never lit;
So we reckon he's a-wrenchin'
Some celestial outlaw's bit.
When the night wind flaps our slickers,
And the rain is cold and stout,
And the lightnin' flares and flickers,
We can sometimes hear him shout:
"I'm a broncho twistin' wonder on the fly;
I'm a ridin' son o' thunder of the sky.
Hey, you earthlin's, shut your winders,
While we're rippin' clouds to flinders.
If this blue-eyed darlin' kicks at you, you die."
Star-dust on his chaps and saddle,
Scornful still of jar and jolt,
He'll come back someday a-straddle
Of a bald-faced thunderbolt;
And the thin-skinned generation
Of that dim and distant day
Sure will stare with admiration
When they hear old Boastful say:
"I was first, as old rawhiders all confessed,
Now I'm the last of all rough riders, and the best.
Huh! you soft and dainty floaters,

With your aeroplanes and motors,
Huh! are you the great-grandchildren of the West?"

—Badger Clark Jr.

The Forgotten City

When with my mother I was coming down
from the country the day of the hurricane,
trees were across the road and small branches
kept rattling on the roof of the car.
There was ten feet or more of water
making the parkways impassable with wind
bringing more rain in sheets. Brown torrents
gushed up through new sluices in the
valley floor so that I had to take what road
I could find bearing to the south and west,
to get back to the city. I passed through
extraordinary places, as vivid as any
I ever saw where the storm had broken
the barrier and let through
a strange commonplace: Long, deserted avenues
with unrecognized names at the corners and
drunken looking people with completely
foreign manners. Monuments, institutions
and in one place a large body of water
startled me with an acre or more of hot
jets spouting up symmetrically over it. Parks.
I had no idea where I was and promised myself
I would some day go back to study this
curious and industrious people who lived
in these apartments, at these sharp
corners and turns of intersecting avenues
with so little apparent communication
with an outside world. How did they get

cut off this way from representation in our
newspapers and other means of publicity
when so near the metropolis, so closely
surrounded by the familiar and the famous?

—*William Carlos Williams*

Old Amusement Park

Before it became LaGuardia Airport.

Hurry, worry, unwary
visitor, never vary
   the pressure till nearly bat-blind.
      A predicament so dire could not
      occur in this rare spot—

where crowds flock to the tramcar
rattling greenish caterpillar,
   as bowling-ball thunder
      quivers the air. The park's elephant
      slowly lies down aslant;

a pygmy replica then rides
the mound the back provides.
   Jet black, a furry pony sits
      down like a dog, has an innocent air—
      no tricks—the best act there.

It's all like the never-ending
Ferris-wheel ascending
   picket-fenced pony-rides (ten cents).
      A businessman, the pony-paddock boy
      locks his equestrian toy—

flags flying, fares collected,
shooting gallery neglected—

half-official, half-sequestered,
limber-slouched against a post,
and tells a friend what matters least.

It's the old park in a nutshell,
like its tame-wild carrousel—
the exhilarating peak
when the triumph is reflective
and confusion, retroactive.

—*Marianne Moore*

Love in America—

Whatever it is, it's a passion—
a benign dementia that should be
engulfing America, fed in a way
   the opposite of the way
in which the Minotaur was fed.
It's a Midas of tenderness;
   from the heart;
nothing else. From one with ability
to bear being misunderstood—
   take the blame, with "nobility
   that is action," identifying itself with
   pioneer unperfunctoriness

   without brazenness or
   bigness of overgrown
   undergrown shallowness.

Whatever it is, let it be without
   affectation.

Yes, yes, yes, *yes.*

         —Marianne Moore

The *Boston Evening Transcript*

The readers of the *Boston Evening Transcript*
Sway in the wind like a field of ripe corn.

When evening quickens faintly in the street,
Wakening the appetites of life in some
And to others bringing the *Boston Evening Transcript,*
I mount the steps and ring the bell, turning
Wearily, as one would turn to nod good-bye to La Rochefoucauld,
If the street were time and he at the end of the street,
And I say, "Cousin Harriet, here is the *Boston Evening Transcript.*"

—*T. S. Eliot*

Dawn in New York

The Dawn! The Dawn! The crimson-tinted, comes
Out of the low still skies, over the hills,
Manhattan's roofs and spires and cheerless domes!
The Dawn! My spirit to its spirit thrills.
Almost the mighty city is asleep,
No pushing crowd, no tramping, tramping feet.
But here and there a few cars groaning creep
Along, above, and underneath the street,
Bearing their strangely-ghostly burdens by,
The women and the men of garish nights,
Their eyes wine-weakened and their clothes awry,
Grotesques beneath the strong electric lights.
The shadows wane. The Dawn comes to New York.
And I go darkly-rebel to my work.

—*Claude McKay*

O Pioneers!

The white sagebrush desert. Noon.
All day heat. But the nights cool. And
Again yellowing dawn. Aspens on
Mountains and yellow sagebrush on sand.

Blind light bewilders. Blown or trampled out,
You cannot follow in the apparent wind
Your father's footsteps. It is to this end
They must have led you. Turn and turn about,

The way is lost to fortune. Forward, back,
Delirium will never find a stream
Running gold sands. Rather the earth will crack
Dry on skeletons, skulls in some daft scheme,

Sockets of eyes that perished crazily,
Ignorant of sun, the sagebrush, mad
Even to the dew. A continent they had
To ravage, and raving romped from sea to sea.

—John Peale Bishop

From a Train Window

Precious in the light of the early sun the Housatonic
Between its not unscalable mountains flows.
Precious in the January morning the shabby fur of the cat-tails by
    the stream.
The farmer driving his horse to the feed-store for a sack of
    cracked corn
Is not in haste; there is no whip in the socket.

Pleasant enough, gay even, by no means sad
Is the rickety graveyard on the hill. Those are not cypress trees
Perpendicular among the lurching slabs, but cedars from the
    neighbourhood,
Native to this rocky land, self-sown. Precious
In the early light, reassuring
Is the grave-scarred hillside.
As if after all, the earth might know what it is about.

—Edna St. Vincent Millay

American Farm, 1934

Space is too full. Did nothing happen here?
Skin of poor life cast off. These pods and shards
Rattle in the old house, rock with the old rocker,
Tick with the old clock, clutter the mantel.
Waste of disregarded trifles crooked as old crochet
On tabourets of wicker. Mute boredom of hoarding
Poor objects. These outlive water sluicing in cracks to
    join
The destroying river, the large Mississippi; or the tornado
Twisting dishes and beds and bird-cages into droppings
    of cloud.
The hard odd thing surviving precariously, once of some
    value
Brought home bright from the store in manila paper,
Now under the foot of the cow, caught in a crevice.
One old shoe, feminine, rotted with damp, one worn tire,
Crop of tin cans, torn harness, nails, links of a chain,—
Edge of a dress, wrappings of contraceptives, trinkets,
Fans spread, sick pink, and a skillet full of mould,
Bottles in cobwebs, butter-nuts—and the copperheads,
Night-feeders, who run their evil bellies in and out
Weaving a fabric of limbo for the devil of limbo;
Droppings of swallows, baked mud of wasps, confetti
Of the mouse nest, ancient cow-dung frozen,
Jumble of items, lost from use, with rusty tools,
Calendars, apple-cores, white sick grasses, gear from the
    stables,
Skull of a cow in the mud, with the stem of dead cabbage,

Part of the spine and the ribs, in the rot of swill mud. This
Array of limbo, once part of swart labor, rusted now,
In every house, in every attic piled. Oh palsied people!
Under the weeds of the outhouse something one never
Picks up or burns; flung away. Let it lie; let it bleach.
Ironic and sinister junk filling a corner. If men vacate,
Prized or unprized, it jests with neglect.
Under the porch the kitten goes and returns,
Masked with small dirt. Odd objects in sheds and shelves,
And the stale air of bed-rooms, stink of stained bureaus,
Flies buzzing in bottles; vocal tone of no meaning.
No wonder our farms are dark and our dreams take these
    shapes.
Thistles mock all, growing out of rubbish
In a heap of broken glass with last year's soot.
Implacable divine rubbish prevails. Possessors of things
Look at the junk heap for an hour. Gnarled idle hands
Find ticks in the pelt of the dog, turn over a plank.
This parasite clutter invades sense and seems to breed
A like in our minds. Wind, water, sun;—it survives.
The whole sad place scales to the thistle and petty litter.
Neglect laughs in the fallen barns and the shutters broken
Hanging on a wailing hinge. Generations of wind
Owe you obeisance. You win. No man will war with you.
He has you in him; his hand trembles; he rights
The front acre while the wife tidies the parlour.
Economy, economy! Who'll till this land?

—*Genevieve Taggard*

Proud Riders

We rode hard, and brought the cattle from brushy springs,
From heavy dying thickets, leaves wet as snow;
From high places, white-grassed and dry in the wind;
Draws where the quaken-asps were yellow and white,
And the leaves spun and spun like money spinning.
We poured them on to the trail, and rode for town.

Men in the fields leaned forward in the wind,
Stood in the stubble and watched the cattle passing.
The wind bowed all, the stubble shook like a shirt.
We threw the reins by the yellow and black fields, and rode,
And came, riding together, into the town
Which is by the gray bridge, where the alders are.
The white-barked alder trees dropping big leaves
Yellow and black, into the cold black water.
Children, little cold boys, watched after us—
The freezing wind flapped their clothes like windmill paddles.
Down the flat frosty road we crowded the herd:
High stepped the horses for us, proud riders in autumn.

—H. L. Davis

"'next to of course god america i"

"next to of course god america i
love you land of the pilgrims' and so forth oh
say can you see by the dawn's early my
country 'tis of centuries come and go
and are no more what of it we should worry
in every language even deafanddumb
thy sons acclaim your glorious name by gorry
by jingo by gee by gosh by gum
why talk of beauty what could be more beaut-
iful than these heroic happy dead
who rushed like lions to the roaring slaughter
they did not stop to think they died instead
then shall the voice of liberty be mute?"

He spoke.   And drank rapidly a glass of water

—*e. e. cummings*

THANKSGIVING (1956)

a monstering horror swallows
this unworld me by you
as the god of our fathers' fathers bows
to a which that walks like a who

but the voice-with-a-smile of democracy
announces night & day
"all poor little peoples that want to be free
just trust in the u s a"

suddenly up rose hungary
and she gave a terrible cry
"no slave's unlife shall murder me
for i will freely die"

she cried so high thermopylae
heard her and marathon
and all prehuman history
and finally The UN

"be quiet little hungary
and do as you are bid
a good kind bear is angary
we fear for the quo pro quid"

uncle sam shrugs his pretty
pink shoulders you know how

and he twitches a liberal titty
and lisps "i'm busy right now"

so rah-rah-rah democracy
let's all be as thankful as hell
and bury the statue of liberty
(because it begins to smell)

—*e. e. cummings*

To Brooklyn Bridge

How many dawns, chill from his rippling rest
The seagull's wings shall dip and pivot him,
Shedding white rings of tumult, building high
Over the chained bay waters Liberty—

Then, with inviolate curve, forsake our eyes
As apparitional as sails that cross
Some page of figures to be filed away;
—Till elevators drop us from our day . . .

I think of cinemas, panoramic sleights
With multitudes bent toward some flashing scene
Never disclosed, but hastened to again,
Foretold to other eyes on the same screen;

And Thee, across the harbor, silver-paced
As though the sun took step of thee, yet left
Some motion ever unspent in thy stride,—
Implicitly thy freedom staying thee!

Out of some subway scuttle, cell or loft
A bedlamite speeds to thy parapets,
Tilting there momently, shrill shirt ballooning,
A jest falls from the speechless caravan.

Down Wall, from girder into street noon leaks,
A rip-tooth of the sky's acetylene;

All afternoon the cloud-flown derricks turn . . .
Thy cables breathe the North Atlantic still.

And obscure as that heaven of the Jews,
Thy guerdon . . . Accolade thou dost bestow
Of anonymity time cannot raise:
Vibrant reprieve and pardon thou dost show.

O harp and altar, of the fury fused,
(How could mere toil align thy choiring strings!)
Terrific threshold of the prophet's pledge,
Prayer of pariah, and the lover's cry,—

Again the traffic lights that skim thy swift
Unfractioned idiom, immaculate sigh of stars,
Beading thy path—condense eternity:
And we have seen night lifted in thine arms.

Under thy shadow by the piers I waited;
Only in darkness is thy shadow clear.
The City's fiery parcels all undone,
Already snow submerges an iron year . . .

O Sleepless as the river under thee,
Vaulting the sea, the prairies' dreaming sod,
Unto us lowliest sometime sweep, descend
And of the curveship lend a myth to God.

—*Hart Crane*

I Like Americans

I like Americans.
They are so unlike Canadians.
They do not take their policemen seriously.
They come to Montreal to drink.
Not to criticize.
They claim they won the war.
But they know at heart that they didn't.
They have such respect for Englishmen.
They like to live abroad.
They do not brag about how they take baths.
But they take them.
Their teeth are so good.
And they wear B.V.D.'s all the year round.
I wish they didn't brag about it.
They have the second best navy in the world.
But they never mention it.
They would like to have Henry Ford for president.
But they will not elect him.
They saw through Bill Bryan.
They have gotten tired of Billy Sunday.
Their men have such funny hair cuts.
They are hard to suck in on Europe.
They have been there once.
They produced Barney Google, Mutt and Jeff.
And Jiggs.
They do not hang lady murderers.
They put them in vaudeville.
They read the Saturday Evening Post

And believe in Santa Claus.
When they make money
They make a lot of money.
They are fine people.

—*Ernest Hemingway*

In Praise
of California Wines

Amid these clear and windy hills
Heat gathers quickly and is gone;
Dust rises, moves, and briefly stills;
Our thought can scarcely pause thereon.

With pale bright leaf and shadowy stem,
Pellucid amid nervous dust,
By pre-Socratic stratagem,
Yet sagging with its weight of must,

The vineyard spreads beside the road
In repetition, point and line.
I sing, in this dry bright abode,
The praises of the native wine.

It yields the pleasure of the eye,
It charms the skin, it warms the heart;
When nights are cold and thoughts crowd high,
Then 'tis the solvent for our art,

When worn for sleep the head is dull,
When art has failed us, far behind,
Its sweet corruption fills the skull
Till we are happy to be blind.

So may I yet, as poets use,
My time being spent, and more to pay,
In this quick warmth the will diffuse,
In sunlight vanish quite away.

—*Yvor Winters*

We're All in the Telephone Book

We're all in the telephone book,
Folks from everywhere on earth—
Anderson to Zabowski,
It's a record of America's worth.

We're all in the telephone book.
There's no priority—
A millionaire like Rockefeller
Is likely to be behind me.

For generations men have dreamed
Of nations united as one.
Just look in your telephone book
To see where that dream's begun.

When Washington crossed the Delaware
And the pillars of tyranny shook,
He started the list of democracy
That's America's telephone book.

—*Langston Hughes*

Sonnet to a Negro in Harlem

You are disdainful and magnificent—
Your perfect body and your pompous gait,
Your dark eyes flashing solemnly with hate,
Small wonder that you are so incompetent
To imitate those whom you so despise—
Your shoulders towering high above the throng,
Your head thrown back in rich, barbaric song,
Palm trees and mangoes stretched before your eyes.
Let others toil and sweat for labor's sake
And wring from grasping hands their meed of gold.
Why urge ahead your supercilious feet?
Scorn will efface each footprint that you make.
I love your laughter arrogant and bold.
You are too splendid for this city street.

—Helene Johnson

Product

There is no beauty in New England like the boats.
Each itself, even the paint white
Dipping to each wave each time
At anchor, mast
And rigging tightly part of it
Fresh from the dry tools
And the dry New England hands.
The bow soars, finds the waves
The hull accepts. Once someone
Put a bowl afloat
And there for all to see, for all the children,
Even the New Englander
Was boatness. What I've seen
Is all I've found: myself.

—*George Oppen*

California

The headland towers over ocean
At Palos Verdes. Who shall say
How the Romantic stood in nature?
But I am sitting in an automobile
While Mary, lovely in a house dress, buys tomatoes from a
    road side stand.

And I look down at the Pacific, blue waves roughly small
    running at the base of land,
An area of ocean in the sun—
Out there is China. Somewhere out in air.
Tree by the stand
Moving in the wind that moves
Streaming with the waves of the Pacific going past.

                The beach: a child
Leaning on one elbow. She has swept an arm
To make a hollow and a mark around her in the sand,
A place swept smooth in one arm's claiming sweep beside
    the ocean,
Looking up the coast relaxed,
A Western child.
And all the air before her—what the wind brings past
In the bright simpleness and strangeness of the sands.

—*George Oppen*

Invitation to Miss Marianne Moore

From Brooklyn, over the Brooklyn Bridge, on this fine morning,
    please come flying.
In a cloud of fiery pale chemicals,
    please come flying,
to the rapid rolling of thousands of small blue drums
descending out of the mackerel sky
over the glittering grandstand of harbor-water,
    please come flying.

Whistles, pennants and smoke are blowing. The ships
are signaling cordially with multitudes of flags
rising and falling like birds all over the harbor.
Enter: two rivers, gracefully bearing
countless little pellucid jellies
in cut-glass epergnes dragging with silver chains.
The flight is safe; the weather is all arranged.
The waves are running in verses this fine morning.
    Please come flying.

Come with the pointed toe of each black shoe
trailing a sapphire highlight,
with a black capeful of butterfly wings and bon-mots,
with heaven knows how many angels all riding
on the broad black brim of your hat,
    please come flying.

Bearing a musical inaudible abacus,
a slight censorious frown, and blue ribbons,
    please come flying.

Facts and skyscrapers glint in the tide; Manhattan
is all awash with morals this fine morning,
     so please come flying.

Mounting the sky with natural heroism,
above the accidents, above the malignant movies,
the taxicabs and injustices at large,
while horns are resounding in your beautiful ears
that simultaneously listen to
a soft uninvented music, fit for the musk deer,
     please come flying.

For whom the grim museums will behave
like courteous male bower-birds,
for whom the agreeable lions lie in wait
on the steps of the Public Library,
eager to rise and follow through the doors
up into the reading rooms,
     please come flying.
We can sit down and weep; we can go shopping,
or play at a game of constantly being wrong
with a priceless set of vocabularies,
or we can bravely deplore, but please
     please come flying.

With dynasties of negative constructions
darkening and dying around you,
with grammar that suddenly turns and shines
like flocks of sandpipers flying,
     please come flying.

Come like a light in the white mackerel sky,
come like a daytime comet
with a long unnebulous train of words,
from Brooklyn, over the Brooklyn Bridge, on this fine morning,
     please come flying.

                    —*Elizabeth Bishop*

Florida

The state with the prettiest name,
the state that floats in brackish water,
held together by mangrove roots
that bear while living oysters in clusters,
and when dead strew white swamps with skeletons,
dotted as if bombarded, with green hummocks
like ancient cannon-balls sprouting grass.
The state full of long S-shaped birds, blue and white,
and unseen hysterical birds who rush up the scale
every time in a tantrum.
Tanagers embarrassed by their flashiness,
and pelicans whose delight it is to clown;
who coast for fun on the strong tidal currents
in and out among the mangrove islands
and stand out on the sand-bars drying their damp gold wings
on sun-lit evenings.
Enormous turtles, helpless and mild,
die and leave their barnacled shells on the beaches,
and their large white skulls with round eye-sockets
twice the size of a man's.
The palm trees clatter in the stiff breeze
like the bills of the pelicans. The tropical rain comes down
to freshen the tide-looped strings of fading shells:
Job's Tear, the Chinese Alphabet, the scarce Junonia,
parti-colored pectins and Ladies' Ears,
arranged as on a gray rag of rotted calico,
the buried Indian Princess's skirt;

with these the monotonous, endless, sagging coast-line
is delicately ornamented.

Thirty or more buzzards are drifting down, down, down,
over something they have spotted in the swamp,
in circles like stirred-up flakes of sediment
sinking through water.
Smoke from woods-fires filters fine blue solvents.
On stumps and dead trees the charring is like black velvet.
The mosquitoes
go hunting to the tune of their ferocious obbligatos.
After dark, the fireflies map the heavens in the marsh
until the moon rises.
Cold white, not bright, the moonlight is coarse-meshed,
and the careless, corrupt state is all black specks
too far apart, and ugly whites; the poorest
post-card of itself.
After dark, the pools seem to have slipped away.
The alligator, who has five distinct calls:
friendliness, love, mating, war, and a warning—
whimpers and speaks in the throat
of the Indian Princess.

—*Elizabeth Bishop*

Tract

Old tract, the houses of wood-siding
Old callas at the drain pipes, a frontal
Cedar, line among lots
Cabs, a wagon, a pick-up
And the bay not far, a dozen miles over town.
A boy on a bike now and again
Makes up a tunafish sandwich and starts off.
Few go out otherwise, they stay in to listen.

For some tracts, a whole range
Of mountains takes the bay's place,
Holds all the answer or loss
Behind curtains as tears.
For some, beyond the outskirts of the houses,
More callas, more houses.

—*Josephine Miles*

The Campaign

My Packard Bell was set up in the vacant lot near the stump
Of the old peach tree. Before it, a love-seat
In tan and green told us what comfort said.
And many looked over us, or sat on the ground, why not?
There certainly were not enough ashtrays for everybody.

And from there it began.
All down the dingle through the mustard ran the voices,
All down the shale in the sunlight ran the faces,
A board fence on the left and a board fence on the right,
Because after all this was private property.

And this is what they said:
He was a child of the people and he will be a man of the people.
He read the Bible at his mother's knee
And that Bible has followed him
All the days of his life.

This is what they said:
The sovereign state of Alabama
Gives you a leader of the people for the people
All the days of his life.
Equal educational opportunity, political opportunity, economic
    opportunity,
Ability, honesty, integrity, widows and orphans.

Canal Zone deems it a privilege
To second the nomination of that great

All the days of his life.
This is what they said. This is what Cooper Blane
Representing the sovereign state of New Jersey said.

Now all the apples in our apple orchard
Are ripening toward fall
And on our poles the beans are greening fast
The pods with sun alert.

And stubble in the field keeps springing yet
In fresh weed, white puffs of daisy weed,
The cat after the gophers
And the breeze brisk.

Round the ears of Packard Bell brisks the breeze
Blows the volume loud and away.
Puffs of volume pile up in the fence corners
Where the cat is active.

What do we understand?
First of all, we know the speakers are speaking the English language.
We can tell that from our love-seat, and others agree.
Second, they are both loud, lively both, and there are two of them.
Who are you for?

Now enters from the upper left, the hill slope,
A dog. After the cat.
For a while we miss the whole campaign,
But later the dog comes round for friendship.
Pats him the taxpayer and the tax receiver.

Now enters from the upper right a fisherman.
He leans to hear what's sounding on the screen
Then wordlessly he fades
Down the green sidepatch and the cliff steps
To the roaring bay, leaving no vote behind.

Ladies and gentlemen, when I spoke to you last
In Pawtucket, Maine, the tide was coming in
With a long roar against the shingle of the world.

And ladies and gentlemen I say to you
Vote now against corruption, calumny,
Crime, evil, and corruption,
For the tide is coming in
With a long foreign roar against the world.
Against Winthrop Rockefeller, fair play,
Farm money, cartels, bourbon, and the fifth districts of the world.

Slowly comes up the moon over Lottie's rabbit shed,
Fencing into the sky its bars of protest,
But the vote midwest moves at another cycle
Of midnight desperate.

South Dakota five no,
Robert J. Martin of the fifth district, no.
And at the four hundred and eightieth slogan
The yes and the yes that will survive the midnight.

One sure thing is
That the tough tubes on this little old Packard Bell
Jiggling and jumping in the twi- and moonlight,
Hot as hornets in the excitement,
Won't set the beans on fire, and won't
Harm the cat, and won't
Even warm us where we sit and listen,
But will burn away
Lively as bugs in the midsummer
To get the last yes and no in the midsummer
On record to the moon's blanched countenance.
Who are you for?

—*Josephine Miles*

Excerpt, The Outer Banks

1

Horizon of islands shifting
Sea-light flame on my voice
burn in me
Light
flows from the water from sands   islands of this horizon
The sea comes toward me across the sea.   The sand
moves over the sand in waves
between the guardians of this landscape
the great commemorative statue on one hand
    —the first flight of man, outside of dream,
        seen as stone wing and stainless steel—
and at the other hand
    banded black-and-white, climbing
the spiral lighthouse.

4

Sands have washed, sea has flown over us.
Between the two guardians, spiral, truncated wing,
history and these wild birds
Bird-voiced discoverers : Hariot,   Hart Crane,
the brothers who watched gulls.
"No bird soars in a calm,"   said Wilbur Wright.
Dragon of the winds forms over me.
Your dance, goddesses in your circle

sea-wreath, whirling of the event
behind me on land as deep in our own lives
we begin to know the movement to come.
Sunken, drowned spirals,
hurricane-dance.

7

Speak to it, says the light.
Speak to it music,
voices of the sea and human throats.
Origins of spirals,
the ballad and original sweet grape
dark on the vines near Hatteras,
tendrils of those vines, whose spiral tower
now rears its light, accompanying
all my voices.

—Muriel Rukeyser

Despisals

In the human cities, never again to
despise the backside of the city, the ghetto,
or build it again as we build the despised
backsides of houses.   Look at your own building.
You are the city.

Among our secrecies, not to despise our Jews
(that is, ourselves) or our darkness, our blacks,
or in our sexuality   wherever it takes us
and we now know we are productive
too productive, too reproductive
for our present invention   —   never to despise
the homosexual who goes building another

with touch   with touch   (not to despise any touch)
each like himself, like herself each.
You are this.

                              In the body's ghetto
never to go despising the asshole
nor the useful shit that is our clean clue
to what we need.   Never to despise
the clitoris in her least speech.

Never to despise in myself what I have been taught
to despise.   Nor to despise the other.
Not to despise the *it*.   To make this relation
with the it : to know that I am it.

—*Muriel Rukeyser*

American Lights,
Seen from off Abroad

Blue go up & blue go down
to light the lights of Dollartown

Nebuchadnezzar had it so good?
wink the lights of Hollywood

I never think, I have so many things,
flash the lights of Palm Springs

I worry like a madwoman over all the world,
affirm the lights, all night, at State

I have no plans, I mean well,
swear the lights of Georgetown

I have the blind staggers
call the lights of Niagara

We shall die in a palace
shout the black lights of Dallas

I couldn't dare less, my favorite son,
fritter the lights of Washington

(I have a brave old So-and-so,
chuckle the lights of Independence, Mo.)

I cast a shadow, what I mean,
blurt the lights of Abilene

Both his sides are all the same
glows his grin with all but shame

'He can do nothing night & day,'
wonder his lovers. So they say.

'Basketball in outer space'
sneers the White New Hampshire House

I'll have a smaller one, later, Mac,
hope the strange lights of Cal Tech

I love you one & all, hate shock,
bleat the lights of Little Rock

I cannot quite focus
cry the lights of Las Vegas

I am a maid of shots & pills,
swivel the lights of Beverly Hills

Proud & odd, you give me vertigo,
fly the lights of San Francisco

I am all satisfied love & chalk,
mutter the great lights of New York

I have lost your way
say the white lights of Boston

Here comes a scandal to blight you to bed.
'Here comes a cropper.' That's what I said.

—*John Berryman*

Southern Song

I want my body bathed again by southern suns, my soul
    reclaimed again from southern land. I want to rest
    again in southern fields, in grass and hay and clover
    bloom; to lay my hand again upon the clay baked by
    a southern sun, to touch the rain-soaked earth and
    smell the smell of soil.

I want my rest unbroken in the fields of southern earth;
    freedom to watch the corn wave silver in the sun and
    mark the splashing of a brook, a pond with ducks
    and frogs and count the clouds.

I want no mobs to wrench me from my southern rest; no
    forms to take me in the night and burn my shack and
    make for me a nightmare full of oil and flame.

I want my careless song to strike no minor key; no fiend to
    stand between my body's southern song—the fusion
    of the South, my body's song and me.

—*Margaret Walker*

The Mouth of the Hudson

A single man stands like a bird-watcher,
And scuffles the pepper and salt snow
from a discarded, gray
Westinghouse Electric cable drum.
He cannot discover America by counting
the chains of condemned freight-trains
from thirty states. They jolt and jar
and junk in the siding below him.
He has trouble with his balance.
His eyes drop,
and he drifts with the wild ice
ticking seaward down the Hudson,
like the blank sides of a jig-saw puzzle.

The ice ticks seaward like a clock.
A Negro toasts
wheat-seeds over the coke-fumes
of a punctured barrel.
Chemical air
sweeps in from New Jersey,
and smells of coffee.

Across the river,
ledges of suburban factories tan
in the sulphur-yellow sun
of the unforgivable landscape.

—*Robert Lowell*

133

We Real Cool

The Pool Players.
Seven at the Golden Shovel.

We real cool. We
Left school. We

Lurk late. We
Strike straight. We

Sing sin. We
Thin gin. We

Jazz June. We
Die soon.

—*Gwendolyn Brooks*

Bronco Busting, Event #1

The stall so tight he can't raise heels or knees
when the cowboy, coccyx to bareback, touches down

tender as a deerfly, forks him, gripping the rope-
handle over the withers, testing the cinch,

as if hired to lift a cumbersome piece of brown
luggage, while assistants perched on the rails arrange

the kicker, a foam-rubber band around the narrowest,
most ticklish part of the loins, leaning full weight

on neck and rump to keep him throttled, this horse,
"Firecracker," jacked out of the box through the sprung

gate, in the same second raked both sides of the belly
by ratchets on booted heels, bursts into five-way

motion: bucks, pitches, swivels, humps, and twists,
an all-over-body-sneeze that must repeat

until the flapping bony lump attached to his spine is gone.
A horn squawks. Up from the dust gets a buster named Tucson.

—May Swenson

Bison Crossing Near Mt. Rushmore

There is our herd of cars stopped,
staring respectfully at the line of bison crossing.
    One big-fronted bull nudges his cow into a run.
She and her calf are first to cross.
    In swift dignity the dark-coated caravan sweeps through
the gap our cars leave in the two-way stall
on the road to the Presidents.
    The polygamous bulls guarding their families from the rear,
the honey-brown calves trotting head-to-hip
by their mothers—who are lean and muscled as bulls,
with chin tassels and curved horns—
all leap the road like a river, and run.
    The strong and somber remnant of western freedom
disappears into the rough grass of the draw,
around the point of the mountain.
    The bison, orderly, disciplined by the prophet-faced,
heavy-headed fathers, threading the pass
of our awestruck stationwagons, Airstreams and trailers,
if in dread of us give no sign,
go where their leaders twine them, over the prairie.
    And we keep to our line,
staring, stirring, revving idling motors, moving
each behind the other, herdlike, where the highway leads.

—May Swenson

The Changing Light

The changing light at San Francisco
        is none of your East Coast light
           none of your
                pearly light of Paris
The light of San Francisco
        is a sea light
           an island light
And the light of fog
        blanketing the hills
        drifting in at night
           through the Golden Gate
              to lie on the city at dawn
And then the halcyon late mornings
        after the fog burns off
        and the sun paints white houses
             with the sea light of Greece
        with sharp clean shadows
        making the town look like
           it had just been painted
But the wind comes up at four o'clock
              sweeping the hills
And then the veil of light of early evening
And then another scrim
        when the new night fog
              floats in

And in that vale of light
　　　　the city drifts
　　　　　　　anchorless upon the ocean

—*Lawrence Ferlinghetti*

vegas

there was a frozen tree that I wanted to paint
but the shells came down
and in Vegas looking across at a green sunshade
at 3:30 in the morning,
I died without nails, without a copy of *The Atlantic Monthly,*
the windows screamed like doves moaning the bombing of Milan
and I went out to live with the rats
but the lights were too bright
and I thought maybe I'd better go back and sit in a
poetry class:

> a marvelous description of a gazelle
> is hell;
> the cross sits like a fly on my window,
> my mother's breath stirs small leaves
> in my mind;

and I hitch-hiked back to L.A. through hangover clouds
and I pulled a letter from my pocket and read it
and the truckdriver said, what's that?
and I said, there's some gal up North who used to
sleep with Pound, she's trying to tell me that H.D.
was our greatest scribe; well, Hilda gave us a few pink
Grecian gods in with the chinaware, but after reading her
I still have 140 icicles hanging from my bones.

I'm not going all the way to L.A., the truckdriver said.

it's all right, I said, the calla lilies nod to our minds
and someday we'll all go home
together.

in fact, he said, this is as far
as we go.
so I let him have it; old withered whore of time
your breasts taste the sour cream of dreaming . . .
he let me out
in the middle of the desert;

to die is to die is to die,

old phonographs in cellars,
joe di maggio,
magazines in with the onions . . .

an old Ford picked me up
45 minutes later
and, this time,
I kept my mouth
shut.

—*Charles Bukowski*

In Georgetown

Holiday Inn, Washington, D.C.

This is not where the rich and famous pursue their lifestyles.
This is exactly like the Holiday Inn in Troy, N.Y., where I stayed recently.
It is near enough to exactly like the Holiday Inn where I stayed in Tucson,
In Casper, in Chillicothe, in Opelika, in Portsmouth, in Bellingham, etc.
A mirror in a fake gilt frame, brass bed lamps attached to the wall by
     hinges.
"Fax Your Urgent Documents To or From This Holiday Inn Hotel."
All at once the smoke alarm goes off for no reason. *Eeeeeeeeeeee!*
Thumps on the door, an anxious black lady. "Are you all right in there, sir?"
I climb on a brocaded chair and disconnect the smoke alarm ruthlessly.
Meanwhile rich and famous men are pursuing their lifestyles two
     blocks away.
In four-story Federal brick houses with porticoes and flagstone steps.
Fucking each other's wives in dens and laundry rooms and pantries.
This is called a party. Some are Democrats, some Republicans, all are
     fuckers.
They are emboldened by bourbon and vodka and the anticipation of
     power.
Tomorrow they will arise hungover and wield the resources of the nation.
Sweetheart, so far from home I'm thinking of you as much as I can.
Melodiously at the door: "Are you all right, sir? Are you all right in there?"

—*Hayden Carruth*

141

Pleasant Avenue

Is in Manhattan
As only those who live there know.

Even the paper-store man is
Italian, Gio. To him even
The *Daily News* delivery
Truckman is mannerly: he
Stops the truck, brings
The corded bundle of papers
Unripped in & sets it on
The maroon-grained plastic seat
Of the dim lunch counter's end stool.
Gio sells and smokes cigars.
I like to watch him unwrap one and
Light it, as if he were
Watching himself.
He sells us mothers malted milk by the
Big tin, cheap, good for li bambini, si.
Men of power gather in his store at night.
My life is so small I feel no fear of them.

The grocer down the block
And the grocer's glowing
Wife shaped like an earth-minder
Sell no potatoes, but stand beside a sea
Of kinds of greens; he lifts from beside
Parsley-tied bunches of uncrimped parsley

A head of escarole, thrusting its gold-to-pale
Center part up from among its shaggy green
To show me, Ecce, I behold.
Glad for his sake I approve. I buy.
His wife allows of me because my babies
Love the very smell of her, & do not whine;
So, nodding, smiling, nervous, he lets me choose
Pears one by one after I sniff at each bottom
Blossom-end to see if they're sweet yet. So far
I have not bruised any of his fruit; in his store
Insofar as I am correct, I am permissible.

East five blocks is the hard
Ware store, outside the invisible
Italian enclave. Here are
Ricani, the laughers; for them
I always wish to be darkly
Much prettier, and elegant.
A capella two men search dueting
For the cement nails I want; I read
Roach killer labels, ant killer
Labels, mouse and rat killer labels;
I glance at kinds of traps and wish
My city had room for more of the less
Desperately alive (despite us)
Withstanders-of-man. But next door
The bodega lady's parrot blazes
Green and thrives!

Brakes on Lexington screech as the
Bodega lady scolds the knife-eyed gang-
Boys and they shuffle; she dares
Send them home to their mothers, sí
Sí, sí, sí, sí, sí, sí, and they go,
Laughing. I'm not afraid of them either.
I have nothing to fear from them
Being I guess afraid only of the loss of love

And of hurting children. And so here
I have nothing to fear.

—*Marie Ponsot*

Wellfleet: The House

Roof overwoven by a soft tussle of leaves,
The walls awave with sumac shadow, lilac
Lofts and falls in the yard, and the house believes
It's guarded, garlanded in a former while.

Here one cannot intrude, the stillness being
Lichenlike grown, a coating of quietudes;
The portraits dream themselves, they are done with seeing;
Rocker and teacart balance in iron moods.

Yet for the transient here is no offense,
Because at certain hours a wallowed light
Floods at the seaside windows, vague, intense,
And lays on all within a mending blight,

Making the kitchen silver blindly gleam,
The yellow floorboards swim, the dazzled clock
Boom with a buoy sound, the chambers seem
Alluvial as that champed and glittering rock.

The sea strokes up to fashion dune and beach
In strew by strew, and year by hundred years.
One is at home here. Nowhere in ocean's reach
Can time have any foreignness or fears.

—*Richard Wilbur*

April and Its Forsythia

It's snowing on the unpedimented lions. On ventilator hoods
white triangles. It evens up wrinkled tar roofs,
smooths out rough concrete coping, showing the shape
of a wall side between coping top and roof. The census
taker was just here. She had on transparent overshoes, coat and
hat: are clothes less secret? Less snowlike?
Snow isn't secret, showing further aspects, how small
cast lions would look if they grew maned, tame yet whitely
fierce; how the center of the sidewalk is always a path
steps tend to, as across a plain, through a wood; how cars
swing out heavily and big at a corner, turning voluminously
as a fleshy dancer. That census taker. I'm the head of a household.
I am also my household. Not bad. It's still snowing, down
and across: when cloth gets old and stretched, a twill
may have a gusty, snowy movement. Rough on poor rats
who work in it, most go out in it: it's dirty cold wet slush
underfoot, you hear it under wheels: swoosh, and slop
when they stop. Mr Merzeg, the super, loves it. Used to drop
to 30 below the nine months he spent in Siberia. There
they really get snow! Not just wet feathers, like New York.
What variety snow falls with and has: this kind lays like wet sheets
or soaked opaque blotting paper: where a surface makes
a natural puddle, its own melting darkens it, as though it had lain
all winter and the thaw is come. Is this change in weather in early April
just what the sugarbush needed, upstate and further up, New Hampshire,
    Vermont?
Maple syrup production is off, the *Times* says, due to the vogue for
    maple furniture.

Willingly or not, you can't give your Cape Cod cobbler's table
with a lamp attachment above a ship's-type wheel back to its grove.
Now it falls on two diagonals, except it's more: the depth dimension
of air. Ugh. The head of this household is going out in it.
Willingly or not, I'll check up on Central Park
where branches of sunshine were in bloom on Monday.

—*James Schuyler*

Bagel Shop Jazz

Shadow people, projected on coffee-shop walls.
Memory formed echoes of a generation past
Beating into now.

Nightfall creatures, eating each other
Over a noisy cup of coffee.

Mulberry-eyed girls in black stockings,
Smelling vaguely of mint jelly and last night's bongo
        drummer,
Making profound remarks on the shapes of navels,
Wondering how the short Sunset week
Became the long Grant Avenue night,
Love tinted, beat angels,
Doomed to see their coffee dreams
Crushed on the floors of time,
As they fling their arrow legs
To the heavens,
Losing their doubts in the beat.

Turtle-neck angel guys, black-haired dungaree guys,
Caesar-jawed, with synagogue eyes,
World travelers on the forty-one bus,
Mixing jazz with paint talk,
High rent, Bartok, classical murders,
The pot shortage and last night's bust.
Lost in a dream world,
Where time is told with a beat.

Coffee-faced Ivy Leaguers, in Cambridge jackets,
Whose personal Harvard was a Fillmore district step,
Weighted down with conga drums,
The ancestral cross, the Othello-laid curse,
Talking of Bird and Diz and Miles,
The secret terrible hurts,
Wrapped in cool hipster smiles,
Telling themselves, under the talk,
This shot must be the end,
Hoping the beat is really the truth.

The guilty police arrive.

Brief, beautiful shadows, burned on walls of night.

—Bob Kaufman

Music

If I rest for a moment near The Equestrian
pausing for a liver sausage sandwich in the Mayflower Shoppe,
that angel seems to be leading the horse into Bergdorf's
and I am naked as a table cloth, my nerves humming.
Close to the fear of war and the stars which have disappeared.
I have in my hands only 35¢, it's so meaningless to eat!
and gusts of water spray over the basins of leaves
like the hammers of a glass pianoforte. If I seem to you
to have lavender lips under the leaves of the world,
        I must tighten my belt.
It's like a locomotive on the march, the season
        of distress and clarity
and my door is open to the evenings of midwinter's
lightly falling snow over the newspapers.
Clasp me in your handkerchief like a tear, trumpet
of early afternoon! in the foggy autumn.
As they're putting up the Christmas trees on Park Avenue
I shall see my daydreams walking by with dogs in blankets,
put to some use before all those coloured lights come on!
        But no more fountains and no more rain,
        and the stores stay open terribly late.

—*Frank O'Hara*

America

America I've given you all and now I'm nothing.
America two dollars and twentyseven cents January
      17, 1956.
I can't stand my own mind.
America when will we end the human war?
Go fuck yourself with your atom bomb.
I don't feel good don't bother me.
I won't write my poem till I'm in my right mind.
America when will you be angelic?
When will you take off your clothes?
When will you look at yourself through the grave?
When will you be worthy of your million Trotskyites?
America why are your libraries full of tears?
America when will you send your eggs to India?
I'm sick of your insane demands.
When can I go into the supermarket and buy what I
      need with my good looks?
America after all it is you and I who are perfect not
      the next world.
Your machinery is too much for me.
You made me want to be a saint.
There must be some other way to settle this argument.
Burroughs is in Tangiers I don't think he'll come back
      it's sinister.
Are you being sinister or is this some form of practical
      joke?
I'm trying to come to the point.
I refuse to give up my obsession.

America stop pushing I know what I'm doing.
America the plum blossoms are falling.
I haven't read the newspapers for months, everyday
        somebody goes on trial for murder.
America I feel sentimental about the Wobblies.
America I used to be a communist when I was a kid
        I'm not sorry.
I smoke marijuana every chance I get.
I sit in my house for days on end and stare at the roses
        in the closet.
When I go to Chinatown I get drunk and never get laid.
My mind is made up there's going to be trouble.
You should have seen me reading Marx.
My psychoanalyst thinks I'm perfectly right.
I won't say the Lord's Prayer.
I have mystical visions and cosmic vibrations.
America I still haven't told you what you did to Uncle
        Max after he came over from Russia.

I'm addressing you.
Are you going to let your emotional life be run by
        Time Magazine?
I'm obsessed by Time Magazine.
I read it every week.
Its cover stares at me every time I slink past the corner
        candystore.
I read it in the basement of the Berkeley Public Library.
It's always telling me about responsibility. Business-
        men are serious. Movie producers are serious.
        Everybody's serious but me.
It occurs to me that I am America.
I am talking to myself again.

Asia is rising against me.
I haven't got a chinaman's chance.
I'd better consider my national resources.
My national resources consist of two joints of
        marijuana millions of genitals an unpublishable

private literature that goes 1400 miles an hour
and twenty-five-thousand mental institutions.
I say nothing about my prisons nor the millions of
underprivileged who live in my flowerpots
under the light of five hundred suns.
I have abolished the whorehouses of France, Tangiers
is the next to go.
My ambition is to be President despite the fact that
I'm a Catholic.

America how can I write a holy litany in your silly
mood?
I will continue like Henry Ford my strophes are as
individual as his automobiles more so they're
all different sexes.
America I will sell you strophes $2500 apiece $500
down on your old strophe
America free Tom Mooney
America save the Spanish Loyalists
America Sacco & Vanzetti must not die
America I am the Scottsboro boys.
America when I was seven momma took me to Com-
munist Cell meetings they sold us garbanzos a
handful per ticket a ticket costs a nickel and the
speeches were free everybody was angelic and
sentimental about the workers it was all so sin-
cere you have no idea what a good thing the
party was in 1835 Scott Nearing was a grand
old man a real mensch Mother Bloor made me
cry I once saw Israel Amter plain. Everybody
must have been a spy.
America you don't really want to go to war.
America it's them bad Russians.
Them Russians them Russians and then Chinamen.
And them Russians.
The Russia wants to eat us alive. The Russia's power
mad. She wants to take our cars from out our
garages.

Her wants to grab Chicago. Her needs a Red *Readers'*
     Digest. Her wants our auto plants in Siberia.
     Him big bureaucracy running our fillingsta-
     tions.
That no good. Ugh. Him make Indians learn read.
     Him need big black niggers. Hah. Her make us
     all work sixteen hours a day. Help.
America this is quite serious.
America this is the impression I get from looking in
     the television set.
America is this correct?
I'd better get right down to the job.
It's true I don't want to join the Army or turn lathes
     in precision parts factories, I'm nearsighted and
     psychopathic anyway.
America I'm putting my queer shoulder to the wheel.

—*Allen Ginsberg*

First Carolina Said-Song

(as told me by an aunt)

In them days
      they won't hardly no way to know if
      somebody way off
      died
          till they'd be
          dead and buried

      and Uncle Jim

hitched up a team of mules to the wagon
and he cracked the whip over them
      and run them their dead-level best
the whole thirty miles to your great grandma's funeral
          down there in
          Green Sea County

          and there come up this
awfulest rainstorm
      you ever saw in your whole life
      and your grandpa

      was setting
      in a goat-skin bottomed chair

and them mules a-running
and him sloshing round in that chairful of water

till he got scalded
he said

and ev-
ery
anch of skin come off his behind:

we got there just in time to see her buried
in an oak grove up
back of the field:

it's growed over with soapbushes and huckleberries now.

—*A. R. Ammons*

Sleet Storm on the Merritt Parkway

I look out at the white sleet covering the still streets
As we drive through Scarsdale—
The sleet began falling as we left Connecticut,
And the winter leaves swirled in the wet air after cars
Like hands suddenly turned over in a conversation.
Now the frost has nearly buried the short grass of March.
Seeing the sheets of sleet untouched on the wide streets,
I think of the many comfortable homes stretching for miles,
Two and three stories, solid, with polished floors,
With white curtains in the upstairs bedrooms,
And small perfume flagons of black glass on the window sills,
And warm bathrooms with guest towels, and electric lights—
What a magnificent place for a child to grow up!
And yet the children end in the river of price-fixing,
Or in the snowy field of the insane asylum.
The sleet falls—so many cars moving toward New York—
Last night we argued about the Marines invading Guatemala in 1947,
The United Fruit Company had one water spigot for 200 families,
And the ideals of America, our freedom to criticize,
The slave systems of Rome and Greece, and no one agreed.

—*Robert Bly*

And One for My Dame

A born salesman,
my father made all his dough
by selling wool to Fieldcrest, Woolrich and Faribo.

A born talker,
he could sell one hundred wet-down bales
of that white stuff. He could clock the miles and sales

and make it pay.
At home each sentence he would utter
had first pleased the buyer who'd paid him off in butter.

Each word
had been tried over and over, at any rate,
on the man who was sold by the man who filled my plate.

My father hovered
over the Yorkshire pudding and the beef:
a peddler, a hawker, a merchant and an Indian chief.

Roosevelt! Willkie! and war!
How suddenly gauche I was
with my old-maid heart and my funny teenage applause.

Each night at home
my father was in love with maps
while the radio fought its battles with Nazis and Japs.

Except when he hid
in his bedroom on a three-day drunk,
he typed out complex itineraries, packed his trunk,

his matched luggage
and pocketed a confirmed reservation,
his heart already pushing over the red routes of the nation.

I sit at my desk
each night with no place to go,
opening the wrinkled maps of Milwaukee and Buffalo,

the whole U.S.,
its cemeteries, its arbitrary time zones,
through routes like small veins, capitals like small stones.

He died on the road,
his heart pushed from neck to back,
his white hanky signaling from the window of his Cadillac.

My husband,
as blue-eyed as a picture book, sells wool:
boxes of card waste, laps and rovings he can pull

to the thread
and say *Leicester, Rambouillet, Merino,*
a half-blood, it's greasy and thick, yellow as old snow.

And when you drive off, my darling,
Yes, sir! Yes, sir! It's one for my dame,
your sample cases branded with my father's name,

your itinerary open,
its tolls ticking and greedy,
its highways built up like new loves, raw and speedy.

—*Anne Sexton*

Transcontinent

Where the cities end, the
dumps grow the oil-can shacks,
from Portland, Maine,

to Seattle. Broken
cars rust in Troy, New York,
and Cleveland Heights.

On the train, the people
eat candy bars, and watch,
or fall asleep.

When they look outside and
see cars and shacks, they know
they're nearly there.

—Donald Hall

Tomorrow

Although the car radio warned that
"war threatened" as "Europe mobilized,"
we set out for the World's Fair on the
last day of August, nineteen-thirty-
nine. My grandparents came visiting
from New Hampshire to Connecticut
once in three years; it wasn't easy
to find somebody to milk the cows,
to feed the hens and sheep: Maybe that's
why we went ahead, with my father
driving down the new Merritt Parkway
toward Long Island. I was ten years old;
for months I had looked forward to this
trip to the Fair. Everywhere I looked
I saw the Trylon and Perisphere—
on ashtrays, billboards, and Dixie Cups;
in *Life*—: those streamlined structures that stood
for The World of Tomorrow, when Dad
would autogyro to pick up Rick
and Judy from a school so modern
it resembled an Airstream trailer.
As we drove home late at night—it was
already morning in Warsaw—I
tried not to let my eyes close. My dear
grandfather—wearing a suit instead
of overalls; my grandmother with
pearls from Newberry's—held my hand tight
in silence. Soon I would fall asleep

as we drove down the Parkway, but first
we stop-and-started through city blocks,
grave in the Pontiac heading north
toward Connecticut, past newsboys
hoarse, dark, and ragged, flapping papers
at the red lights of intersections.

—*Donald Hall*

Belle Isle, 1949

We stripped in the first warm spring night
and ran down into the Detroit River
to baptize ourselves in the brine
of car parts, dead fish, stolen bicycles,
melted snow. I remember going under
hand in hand with a Polish highschool girl
I'd never seen before, and the cries
our breath made caught at the same time
on the cold, and rising through the layers
of darkness into the final moonless atmosphere
that was this world, the girl breaking
the surface after me and swimming out
on the starless waters towards the lights
of Jefferson Ave. and the stacks
of the old stove factory unwinking.
Turning at last to see no island at all
but a perfect calm dark as far
as there was sight, and then a light
and another riding low out ahead
to bring us home, ore boats maybe, or smokers
walking alone. Back panting
to the gray coarse beach we didn't dare
fall on, the damp piles of clothes,
and dressing side by side in silence
to go back where we came from.

—*Philip Levine*

Prospective Immigrants Please Note

Either you will
go through this door
or you will not go through.

If you go through
there is always the risk
of remembering your name.

Things look at you doubly
and you must look back
and let them happen.

If you do not go through
it is possible
to live worthily

to maintain your attitudes
to hold your position
to die bravely

but much will blind you,
much will evade you,
at what cost who knows?

The door itself
makes no promises.
It is only a door.

—*Adrienne Rich*

Excerpt, From an Old House in America

7.

I am an American woman:
I turn that over

like a leaf pressed in a book
I stop and look up from

into the coals of the stove
or the black square of the window

Foot-slogging through the Bering Strait
jumping from the *Arbella* to my death

chained to the corpse beside me
I feel my pains begin

I am washed up on this continent
shipped here to be fruitful

my body a hollow ship
bearing sons to the wilderness

sons who ride away
on horseback, daughters

whose juices drain like mine
into the *arroyo* of stillbirths, massacres

Hanged as witches, sold as breeding-wenches
my sisters leave me

I am not the wheatfield
nor the virgin forest

I never chose this place
yet I am of it now

In my decent collar, in the daguerrotype
I pierce its legend with my look

my hands wring the necks of prairie chickens
I am used to blood

When the men hit the hobo track
I stay on with the children

my power is brief and local
but I know my power

I have lived in isolation
from other women, so much

in the mining camps, the first cities
the Great Plains winters

Most of the time, in my sex, I was alone

—*Adrienne Rich*

All over the Dry Grasses

Motorburn,   oil sump dirt smell
          brake   drum
once deer kisst, grazed, pranct,
                pisst,
all over
California.

household laps.   gum tea
          buds.
     new houses,
     found wed on block pie.

sa.
bring back thick walls,
     (cools my poison,
               poison,
          scorpio itch, tick—)

     dreaming of

          babies

All over Mendocino County
wrappt in wild iris
          leaves.

               —*Gary Snyder*

Every Traveler Has One Vermont Poem

Spikes of lavender aster under Route 91
hide a longing or confession
"I remember when air was invisible"
from Chamberlain Hill down to Lord's Creek
tree mosses point the way home.

Two nights of frost
and already the hills are turning
curved green against the astonished morning
sneeze-weed and ox-eye daisies
not caring   I am a stranger
making a living choice.

Tanned boys I do not know
on their first proud harvest
wave from their father's tractor
one smiles as we drive past
the other hollers
nigger
into cropped and fragrant air.

—*Audre Lorde*

Listenen to Big Black at S.F. State

no mo meetings
where u talk bout
whitey. the cracker
who done u wrong
           (like some sad/bitch
who split in the middle of yo/comen)
just.   gitting.   stronNNNger.
                      maken warriors
outa boys.
      blk/woooomen
           outa girls.
              moven in &
out of blkness
       till it runs this
           400/yr/old/road/show
(called
     amurica.
       now liven off its re/runs.)
            off the road.
no mo tellen the man he is
         a dead/die/en/motha/
fucka.
     just a sound of drums.
            the sonnnnnNNg of chiefs
pouren outa our blk/sections.
     aree-um-doo-doo-doooooo-WORK
     aree-um-doo-doo-doooooo-LOVE
     arem-doooo-UNITY

arem-doooo-LAND
arem-doooo-WAR
arem-doooo-BUILDEN

aree-um-doo-doo-dooooo. MalcolMmmm
aree-um-doo-doo-dooooo. ElijahHHH
aree-um-doo-doo-dooooo. Imamuuuu

just the sonnnng of chiefs.
loud with blk/nation/hood
builden.

—*Sonia Sanchez*

American Twilight

Why do I love the sound of children's voices in unknown games
So much on a summer's night,
Lightning bugs lifting heavily out of the dry grass
Like alien spacecraft looking for higher ground,
Darkness beginning to sift like coffee grains

over the neighborhood?

Whunk of a ball being kicked,
Surf-suck and surf-spill from traffic along the bypass,
American twilight,

Venus just lit in the third heaven,
Time-tick between "Okay, let's go," and "This earth is not my
    home."

Why do I care about this? Whatever happens will happen
With or without us,

with or without these verbal amulets.
In the first ply, in the heaven of the moon, a little light,
Half-light, over Charlottesville.
Trees reshape themselves, the swallows disappear, lawn sprinklers
    do the wave.

Nevertheless, it's still summer: cicadas pump their boxes,
Jack Russell terriers, as they say, start barking their heads off,
And someone, somewhere, is putting his first foot, then the second,
Down on the other side,

no hand to help him, no tongue to wedge its weal.

—*Charles Wright*

at the cemetery, walnut grove plantation, south carolina, 1989

among the rocks
at walnut grove
your silence drumming
in my bones,
tell me your names.

nobody mentioned slaves
and yet the curious tools
shine with your fingerprints.
nobody mentioned slaves
but somebody did this work
who had no guide, no stone,
who moulders under rock.

tell me your names,
tell me your bashful names
and i will testify.

the inventory lists ten slaves
but only men were recognized.

among the rocks
at walnut grove
some of these honored dead
were dark
some of these dark

were slaves
some of these slaves
were women
some of them did this
honored work.
tell me your names
foremothers, brothers,
tell me your dishonored names.
here lies
here lies
here lies
here lies
hear

—*Lucille Clifton*

black power poem

a spectre is haunting america—the spectre of hoodooism .
all the powers of old america have entered into a holy
    alli
ance to exorcise this spectre : allen ginsberg timothy
    leary
richard nixon richard daley time magazine the new york
    review
of books and the underground press .
may the best church win . shake hands now and come
out conjuring

—Ishmael Reed

Iowa

Air as the fuel of owls. Snow
unravels, its strings slacken. Creamed

to a pulp are those soft gongs
clouds were. The children

with minds moist as willow pile
clouds purely in their minds; thrones

throng on a bright mud strangely
shining. And here

chase a hog home as a summer sun
rambles over the pond, and here run

under a sky ancient as America with
its journeying clouds. All their hands

are ferns and absences. Their farm homes
on their hills are strangely childlike.

—*Michael Dennis Browne*

Why We Are Truly a Nation

Because we rage inside
the old boundaries,
like a young girl leaving the Church,
scared of her parents.

Because we all dream of saving
the shaggy, dung-caked buffalo,
shielding the herd with our bodies.

Because grief unites us,
like the locked antlers of moose
who die on their knees in pairs.

—*William Matthews*

Knoxville, Tennessee

I always like summer
best
you can eat fresh corn
from daddy's garden
and okra
and greens
and cabbage
and lots of
barbecue
and buttermilk
and homemade ice-cream
at the church picnic
and listen to
gospel music
outside
at the church
homecoming
and go to the mountains with
your grandmother
and go barefooted
and be warm
all the time
not only when you go to bed
and sleep

—*Nikki Giovanni*

My Poem

i am 25 years old
black female poet
wrote a poem asking
nigger can you kill
if they kill me
it won't stop
the revolution

i have been robbed
it looked like they knew
that i was to be hit
they took my tv
my two rings
my piece of african print
and my two guns
if they take my life
it won't stop
the revolution

my phone is tapped
my mail is opened
they've caused me to turn
on all my old friends
and all my new lovers
if i hate all black
people
and all negroes
it won't stop

if I never write
another poem
or short story
if i flunk out
of grad school
if my car is reclaimed
and my record player
won't play
and if i never see
a peaceful day
or do a meaningful
black thing

the revolution

i'm afraid to tell
my roommate where i'm going
and scared to tell
people if i'm coming
if i sit here
for the rest
of my life
it won't stop
the revolution

it won't stop
the revolution

the revolution
is in the streets
and if i stay on
the 5th floor
it will go on
if i never do
anything
it will go on

—*Nikki Giovanni*

179

Today I Am a Homicide
in the North of the City

on this bus to oblivion i bleed in the seat
numb silent rider
bent to poverty/my blackness covers me like the
american flag over the coffin of some hero killed in action
unlike him i have remained unrecognized, unrewarded
eyes cloaked in the shroud of hopelessness
search advancing avenues for a noisy haven
billboards press against my face
reminders of what i can't afford to buy
laughing fantasies speed past in molded steel luxury
i get off at a dark corner
and in my too tight slacks
move into the slow graceful mood of shadow

i know my killer is out there

—*Wanda Coleman*

Walking Back Up Depot Street

In Hollywood, California (she'd been told) women travel
on roller skates, pull a string of children, grinning, gaudy-
eyed as merry-go-round horses, brass wheeled
under a blue canopy of sky.

                           Beatrice had never
lived in such a place. This morning, for instance, beside
Roxboro Road, she'd seen a woman with no feet wheel
her chair into fragile clumps of new grass. Her legs ended
at the ankle, old brown cypress knees. She furrowed herself
by hand through the ground. Cars passed. The sky stared down.
At the center of the world's blue eye, the woman stared back.

Years revolved, began to circle Beatrice, a ring of burning eyes.
They flared and smoked like the sawmill fires she walked past

     as a child, in the afternoon at 4 o'clock, she and a dark woman,
     past the cotton gin, onto the bridge above the railroad tracks.
     There they waited for wheels to rush like the wings of an iron angel,
     for the white man at the engine to blow the whistle. Beatrice had waited
     to stand in the tremble of power.

                          Thirty years later she saw
the scar, the woman who had walked beside her then, split
but determined to live, raising mustard greens to get through
the winter. Whether she had, this spring, Beatrice did not know.
If she was sitting, knotted feet to the stove, if the coal had lasted,

if she cared for her company, pictures under table glass,
the eyes of children she had raised for others.

                         If Beatrice went back
to visit at her house, sat unsteady in a chair in the smoky room,
they'd be divided by past belief, the town's parallel tracks,
people never to meet even in distance. They would be joined
by the memory of walking back up Depot Street.

                         She could sit
and say: *I have changed, have tried to replace the iron heart*
with a heart of flesh.

                But the woman whose hands had washed her,
had pulled a brush through her hair, whose hands had brought her maypops,
the green fruit and purple flowers, fierce eyes of living creatures—
What had she given her, that woman, anything all these years?

Words would not remake the past. She could not make it
vanish like an old photograph thrown onto live coals.

If she meant to live in the present, she would have to work, do
without, send money, call home long distance about the heat.

                —*Minnie Bruce Pratt*

At the Public Market Museum:
Charleston, South Carolina

A volunteer, a Daughter of the Confederacy,
receives my admission and points the way.
Here are gray jackets with holes in them,
red sashes with individual flourishes,
things soft as flesh. Someone sewed
the gold silk cord onto that gray sleeve
as if embellishments
could keep a man alive.

I have been reading *War and Peace,*
and so the particulars of combat
are on my mind—the shouts and groans
of men and boys, and the horses' cries
as they fall, astonished at what
has happened to them.
                        Blood on leaves,
blood on grass, on snow; extravagant
beauty of red. Smoke, dust of disturbed
earth; parch and burn.

Who would choose this for himself?
And yet the terrible machinery
waited in place. With psalters
in their breast pockets, and gloves
knitted by their sisters and sweethearts,
the men in gray hurled themselves

out of the trenches, and rushed against
blue. It was what both sides
agreed to do.

—*Jane Kenyon*

The Way Things Are in Franklin

Even the undertaker is going out
of business. And since the dime store closed,
we can't get parakeets on Main Street
anymore, or sleeveless gingham smocks
for keeping Church Fair pie off the ample
fronts of the strong, garrulous wives
of pipefitters and road agents.
The hardware's done for too.
                                    Yesterday,
a Sunday, I saw the proprietors breaking
up shop, the woman struggling with half
a dozen bicycle tires on each arm,
like bangle bracelets, the man balancing
boxes filled with Teflon pans. The windows
had been soaped to frustrate curiosity,
or pity, or that cheerless satisfaction
we sometimes feel when others fail.

—*Jane Kenyon*

American Trains

The Santa Fe, still the one
    that most often sings me its name;
and the rattling Erie & Lackawanna
    that used to ride my first love—
    in whose bed I cried with the thought
    no days would ever be long enough for us—
    to Pennsylvania and school, far
    before I had tried her attention,
    truly, or her forgiveness;
and the always late AMTRAK Montrealer
    that stopped in Massachusetts cornfields
    one night to wait for all the stars
    and American clocks to catch up to it
    as Daylight Savings came on;
and the smoky Conrail commuter
    that rocked and screeched through chemical air
    to New York, a rolling lurching urinal
    carrying bankers and middlemen
    and secretaries smoothing
    their weekday best and putting new lipstick on
    as we coasted out of the tunnel
    into Penn Station and waited—standing
    jammed together with salesmen whose sportcoats
    would never hang right from their tired shoulders,
    and teachers needing new heels, and lawyers—
    waited for the doors to open onto the hot black platform;
and the relic locomotive and open cars
    careening a few miles for tourists in New Jersey,

the steam engine shocking eyes
with smoke and coal motes, flushing pheasants
gaudy with mating out of the trackside brush
on the back side of shopping centers;
and there's the one you and I got on,
that started downhill with the weight
of what we felt and is still in a plummet,
always and always faster till it has us shaking,
out of breath, scared . . . "A *freight* train,"
I said when you asked me, "What *is* this?"

—*Reginald Gibbons*

Facing It

My black face fades,
hiding inside the black granite.
I said I wouldn't,
dammit: No tears.
I'm stone. I'm flesh.
My clouded reflection eyes me
like a bird of prey, the profile of night
slanted against morning. I turn
this way—the stone lets me go.
I turn that way—I'm inside
the Vietnam Veterans Memorial
again, depending on the light
to make a difference.
I go down the 58,022 names,
half-expecting to find
my own in letters like smoke.
I touch the name Andrew Johnson;
I see the booby trap's white flash.
Names shimmer on a woman's blouse
but when she walks away
the names stay on the wall.
Brushstrokes flash, a red bird's
wings cutting across my stare.
The sky. A plane in the sky.
A white vet's image floats
closer to me, then his pale eyes
look through mine. I'm a window.
He's lost his right arm

inside the stone. In the black mirror
a woman's trying to erase names:
No, she's brushing a boy's hair.

—*Yusef Komunyakaa*

Language Lesson 1976

When Americans say a man
takes liberties, they mean

he's gone too far. In Philadelphia today I saw
a kid on a leash look mom-ward

and announce his fondest wish: one
bicentennial burger, hold

the relish. Hold is forget,
in America.

On the courts of Philadelphia
the rich prepare

to serve, to fault. The language is a game as well,
in which love can mean nothing,

doubletalk mean lie. I'm saying
doubletalk with me. I'm saying

go so far the customs are untold.
Make nothing without words,

and let me be
the one you never hold.

—Heather McHugh

Queens, 1963

Everyone seemed more American
than we, newly arrived,
foreign dirt still on our soles.
By year's end, a sprinkler waving
like a flag on our mowed lawn,
we were melted into the block,
owned our own mock Tudor house.
Then the house across the street
sold to a black family.
Cop cars patrolled our block
from the Castellucci's at one end
to the Balakian's on the other.
We heard rumors of bomb threats,
a burning cross on their lawn.
(It turned out to be a sprinkler.)
Still the neighborhood buzzed.
The barber's family, Haralambides,
our left side neighbors, didn't want trouble.
They'd come a long way to be free!
Mr. Scott, the retired plumber,
and his plump midwestern wife,
considered moving back home
where white and black got along
by staying where they belonged.
They had cultivated our street
like the garden she'd given up
on account of her ailing back,
bad knees, poor eyes, arthritic hands.

She went through her litany daily.
Politely, my mother listened—
¡Ay, Mrs. Scott, qué pena!
—her Dominican good manners
still running on automatic.
The Jewish counselor next door,
had a practice in her house;
clients hurried up her walk
ashamed to be seen needing.
(I watched from my upstairs window,
gloomy with adolescence,
and guessed how they too must have
hypocritical old world parents.)
Mrs. Bernstein said it was time
the neighborhood opened up.
As the first Jew on the block,
she remembered the snubbing she got
a few years back from Mrs. Scott.
But real estate worried her,
our houses' plummeting value.
She shook her head as she might
at a client's grim disclosures.
Too bad the world works this way.
The German girl playing the piano
down the street abruptly stopped
in the middle of a note.
I completed the tune in my head
as I watched *their* front door open.
A dark man in a suit
with a girl about my age
walked quickly into a car.
My hand lifted but fell
before I made a welcoming gesture.
On her face I had seen a look
from the days before we had melted
into the United States of America.
It was hardness mixed with hurt.
It was knowing she never could be

the right kind of American.
A police car followed their car.
Down the street, curtains fell back.
Mrs. Scott swept her walk
as if it had just been dirtied.
Then the German piano commenced
downward scales as if tracking
the plummeting real estate.
One by one I imagined the houses
sinking into their lawns,
the grass grown wild and tall
in the past tense of this continent
before the first foreigners owned
any of this free country.

—*Julia Alvarez*

California Dreamin'

Was I this lonely as a child
My bones are lonely now.
Pointing to a white flag with a brown bear on it
the teacher tells us this is our state flag.
In my class everybody is born in America.
We pledge allegiance to the flag
of the United States.
The teacher tells us the Sequoia is our state tree
that they are the tallest trees in the world.
I wonder about a boy I knew in kindergarten
so short he had trouble climbing into
his seat. Is he lonely now like
a ferris wheel abandoned in the rain.
As a child I liked those things—ferris wheels,
cotton candy, crinolines, the Mouseketeers.
I wonder was my brother always lonely? Ever?
Was he lonely in the park when the killer came?
When god erased his name could he feel it,
was he lonely?
Was he cold the night, the years, he walked alone?
Did he think about his childhood? Did he think
he was insane?
Did the voices writing in the wind
comfort him or drive him like a shepherd
over concrete collecting aluminum cans?
Did he breathe his own blood like a blanket finally
covering him?

Can we lay down together now like I always wanted
     since
I am so lonely and he is bones?
The Golden Poppy is our state flower.
California is the second largest state in the Union.
The teacher? Where is she now?
Is she old? Dead? Did she die from drinking
or complete twenty-five years of talking to lonely
     desperate
old people in baby bodies about the kinds
of clouds, arithmetic, verbs, George Washington.
Did she know we would end up rainy eyes,
homeless, wandering through state forests
trying to find the trees she taught us were ours?

—*Sapphire*

The Dream Life of a Coffin Factory
in Lynn, Massachusetts

Earlier in the century it was not unusual to spend an evening
        on the verandah.
It was a time when movie theaters sprawled around
newly constructed lagoons, their blue concrete walls
rising out of Wisconsin snow drifts, their tile roofs
fiercely gathering Delaware's wind-swept soot in March.

Every street personalized its drugstore with mahogany stools
on which one could perch, and wait for evening to unfold its
        newspaper, shake out its umbrella.
And at night, long after everyone was asleep,
the rows of chrome spigots still glistened with pride.

Now it was dusk; and floating above these warm suburbs
was a tremendous dome, whose perimeter was molded
with high relief figures of motorcycles and pouting dancers,
wagon wheels and other things classical.

In Wisconsin's lagoons it was still considered graceful
for a man to sit in a drugstore and wait for a hand
        to squeeze an orange pill.

In Delaware's soot a woman could sit on a wall
and lose hours counting clouds unfolding
        in the darkness.

It was, if anything, a newly constructed century—
a time when only motorcycles sprawled fiercely
                in the rain.

Behind the movie theater a warm glow spread out
from the window of the hacienda, bravely gathering
the remnants of evening to its yellow handkerchief.

Even the narrower streets had their own lagoons,
each one lined with stucco clouds on which one could sleep,
waiting for evening to deliver its pastel uniforms.
It would remain an evening of waiting,
for men and women floated above the suburbs,
pouting fiercely in the last stages of a withered century.

In March, in Wisconsin, young men shed their mustaches.
                After carefully weighing them,
they were placed in linen handkerchiefs and buried in the snow.
In the evening they ran back to the classical suburbs,
where rows of young women leaned in glistening drugstores,
waiting for the clouds to get older.

The perimeter of these suburbs was carefully outlined
                by chrome spigots.
Lawns rose fiercely out of the snow, while paper bags
                seldom crossed the avenue.
If a newspaper floated past a window, a pale hand clutched
            · a withered foot.
It was a time when the century had gone to sleep,
and everyone glistened with pride.

                —*John Yau*

Community Garden,
Sixth Street and Avenue B

Into this urban outback
      a child could simply disappear,
           join the feral cats
               scaling the Rococo jumble

of three-by-fours.
      The tabbies have the leisure
           to peruse the encyclopedic
               toy store of discards—

kiddie pool, beach ball,
      Star Trek punching bag—
           aloft on wires behind the iron gate.
               Perpendicular to the forty-foot scaffolding

hangs the plastic horse
      that bucked for a quarter
           at Woolworth's Five-and-Dime. Released
               from memory's corral, she gazes

toward the rearing merry-go-round pony,
      carved in a car barn in Brooklyn, 1925,
           rosettes and tassels decorating the saddle,
               still galloping to Coney Island.

What gives this tiered tree house
        its wacky, broken wickedness?
                The tawdry and the classical hydroplane
                    the late September morning

and I cannot, for once, sprint past
        this pyramid of junk, this towering irony
                without noticing Dumbo, mouth full of shark teeth,
                    sailing into the cartoon sky.

                    —*Robin Becker*

Crab-Boil

(Ft. Myers, 1962)

Why do I remember the sky
above the forbidden beach,
why only blue and the scratch,
shell on tin, of their distress?
The rest

imagination supplies:
bucket and angry pink beseeching
claws. Why does Aunt Helen
laugh before saying "Look at that—

a bunch of niggers, not
a-one get out 'fore the others pull him
back." I don't believe her—

just as I don't believe *they* won't come
and chase us back to the colored-only shore
crisp with litter and broken glass.

"When do we kill them?"
"Kill 'em? Hell, the water does *that.*
They don't feel a thing . . . no nervous system."

I decide to believe this: I'm hungry.
Dismantled, they're merely exotic,

a blushing meat. After all, she *has*
grown old in the South. If
we're kicked out now, I'm ready.

—*Rita Dove*

Silos

Like martial swans in spring paraded against the city sky's
shabby blue, they were always too white and
suddenly there.

They were never fingers, never xylophones, although once
a stranger said they put him in mind of Pan's pipes
and all the lost songs of Greece. But to the townspeople
they were like cigarettes, the smell chewy and bitter
like a field shorn of milkweed, or beer brewing, or
a fingernail scorched over a flame.

No, no, exclaimed the children. They're a fresh packet of chalk,
dreading math work.

They were masculine toys. They were tall wishes. They
were the ribs of the modern world.

—*Rita Dove*

I Hear the Bells of the Ice-Cream Vendor Outside My Door

The sign on his cart says *Pancho's Ice Cream.*
Pifas, my cousin, beats me to the raspa treats,

the ice-cream vendor pushing his cart as I cross the bridge.
The wind knocks me over, lifts me near the cliffs.

A thousand feet below, purple rocks take me
farther away from my early streets.

The sign appears again—Pancho's Ice Cream.
I hear the bells and his cries, *"Paletas! Paletas!"*

The man pushes his cart, leaves me hanging
off the bridge, a tornado striking my mother's house,

ice from snowcones flying across the chasm of fear
as I reach the other side of the bridge.

I wake in the trees of a flavor I never tasted,
my lost cousin dead in Vietnam, bells of the vendor

ringing in my ears as I buy two snowcones—
one for Pifas, one for me, and I eat mine

in darkness as the second drips
strawberry red in my cold hands.

—*Ray Gonzalez*

Adonis Theater

It must have seemed the apex of dreams,
the movie palace on Eighth Avenue
with its tiered chrome ticket-booth,
Tibetan, the phantom blonde head

of the cashier floating
in its moon window. They'd outdone each other
all over the neighborhood, raising
these blunt pastiches of anywhere

we couldn't go: a pagoda, a future,
a Nepal. The avenue fed into the entry
with its glass cases of radiant stars,
their eyes dreamy and blown

just beyond human proportions to prepare us
for how enormous they would become inside,
after the fantastic ballroom of the lobby,
when the uniformed usher would show the way

to seats reserved for us in heaven.
I don't know when it closed,
or if it ever shut down entirely,
but sometime—the forties?—

they stopped repainting the frescoes,
and when the plaster fell they merely

swept it away, and allowed
the gaps in the garlands of fruit

that decked the ceiling above the second balcony.
The screen shrunk to a soiled blank
where these smaller films began to unreel,
glorifying not the face but the body.

Or rather, bodies, ecstatic
and undifferentiated as one film ends
and the next begins its brief and awkward exposition
before it reaches the essential

matter of flesh. No one pays much attention
to the screen. The viewers wander
in the steady, generous light washing back
up the long aisles toward the booth.

Perhaps we're hurt by becoming
beautiful in the dark, whether we watch
Douglas Fairbanks escaping from a dreamed,
suavely oriental city—think of those leaps

from the parapet, how he almost flies
from the grasp of whatever would limit him—
or the banal athletics of two or more men who were
and probably remain strangers. Perhaps

there's something cruel in the design
of the exquisite plaster box
built to frame the exotic
and call it desirable. When the show's over,

it is, whether it's the last frame
of Baghdad or the impossibly extended
come shot. And the solitary viewers,
the voyeurs and married men go home,

released from the swinging chrome doors
with their splendid reliefs
of the implements of artistry,
released into the streets as though washed

in something, marked with some temporary tattoo
that will wear away on the train ride home,
before anyone has time to punish them for it.
Something passing, even though the blood,

momentarily, has broken into flower
in the palace of limitless desire—
how could one ever be *done* with a god?
All its illusion conspires,

as it always has, to show us one another
in this light, whether we look to
or away from the screen.

—*Mark Doty*

Spiderman Versus the Kachinas

The Hopis in Shungopovi have closed their annual
Powamu kachina dances to whites this year.
Armed tribal police block the dirt road to the pueblo
with their jeeps to enforce the ban.

Several different Hopis told Nicole and I
that last year Marvel Comics put out a comic book
depicting kachinas
(The Hopis sacred supernatural and ancestral spirits)
as evil monsters.
The bad guys for some white superhero to fight
in order to save the world.

Outside a small adobe house in the pueblo of Walpi,
a homemade sign hanging in the window advertised
kachina dolls for sale.
Inside a young Hopi boy was drawing
and coloring in a notebook at a wooden table.
He wore a L.A. Raiders t-shirt
and was listening to a tape of Hopi vocal music.
Without smiling, he showed us two small kachina dolls
and when we said we weren't interested in buying them,
he shrugged and went back to his notebook.

Nicole and I couldn't help but notice that he was drawing
Marvel Comic's superhero, Spiderman.

IS SPIDERMAN YOUR HERO? Nicole asked him.

YES, HE IS. The Hopi boy said, still not smiling.

—*Dave Alvin*

The Hula Skirt, 1959

Before my fourth birthday my father
and (what I didn't know) my pregnant mother and I
flew through clouds and over silos and barns
to Disneyland and a motel
where I locked a restaurant bathroom stall
and crawled out under the door for fun
and chose the Peter Pan ride the only ride I recall
I recall as a yellow seat and closed eyes
then flew to Honolulu then Maui
where we drove between the cane plantations
that I would later watch burn in harvesting
its sweet pithy wrist
to my grandmother drying her hands and opening her arms
to meet my almost Japanese face,
the chickens clucking to get in the way it seemed,
and I felt shy around grandfather's wheel chair
and empty mouth. A baby's grin.
Then it was my birthday that I'd waited for since my third one
and mom brought out a store-bought cake
(Mama, too hot to bake, she insisted)
that was pink and I had many packages
including a brown-skinned doll wearing a muu-muu
and in the last funny-shaped one
an orchid-print bra and hula skirt.
They wrapped it around my tiny, pale waist
adjusted the top and said, smile Kimi,
for this snapshot of banana trees and me.
Two pack-rats, this hula skirt has survived these thirty years

to land in my even smaller New York apartment
where my daughter will take it for show-and-tell
and sing something my mother taught her that begins with aloha
and is about the humuhumu nukunuku apua that go swimming by.
That much I remember.

—*Kimiko Hahn*

What the Janitor Heard in the Elevator

The woman in gold bracelets tells her friend:
I had to fire another one.
Can you believe it?
She broke the vase
Jack gave me for Christmas.
It was one of those,
you know? That worked
with everything. All my colors.
I asked him if he'd mind
if I bought one again just like it.
It was the only one that just always worked.

Her friend says:
Find another one that speaks English.
That's a plus.

The woman in gold agrees
that is a plus.

—*Barbara Kingsolver*

Eden

Yellow-oatmeal flowers of the windmill palms
like brains lashed to fans—
even they think of cool paradise, .

not this sterile air-conditioned chill
or the Arizona hell in which they sway becomingly.
Every time I return to Phoenix I see these palms

as a child's height marks on a kitchen wall,
taller now than the yuccas they were planted with,
taller than the Texas sage trimmed

to a perfect gray-green globe with pointillist
lavender blooms, taller than I,
who stopped growing years ago and commenced instead

my slow, almost imperceptible slouch
to my parents' old age:
Father's painful bend—really a bending of a bend—

to pick up the paper at the end of the sidewalk;
Mother, just released from Good Samaritan,
curled sideways on a sofa watching the soaps,

an unwanted tear inching down
at the plight of some hapless Hilary or Tiffany.
How she'd rail against television as a waste of time!

Now, with one arthritis-mangled hand,
she aims the remote control at the set
and flicks it off in triumph, turning to me

as I turn to the tree framed in the Arcadia door.
Her smile of affection melts into the back of my head,
a throb that presses me forward,

hand pressed to glass. I feel the desert heat
and see the beautiful shudders of the palms in the yard
and wonder why I despised this place so,

why I moved from city to temperate city, anywhere
without palms and cactus trees.
I found no paradise, as my parents know,

but neither did they, with their eager sprinklers
and scrawny desert plants pumped up to artificial splendor,
and their lives sighing away, exhaling slowly,

the man and woman
who teach me now as they could not before
to prefer real hell to any imaginary paradise.

—*David Woo*

Boston Year

My first year in Cambridge a car full of white boys
tried to run me off the road, and spit through the window,
open to ask directions. I was always asking directions
and always driving: to an Armenian market
in Watertown to buy figs and string cheese, apricots,
dark spices and olives from barrels, tubes of paste
with unreadable Arabic labels. I ate
stuffed grape leaves and watched my lips swell in the mirror.
The floors of my apartment would never come clean.
Whenever I saw other colored people
in bookshops, or museums, or cafeterias, I'd gasp,
smile shyly, but they'd disappear before I spoke.
What would I have said to them? Come with me? Take
me home? Are you my mother? No. I sat alone
in countless Chinese restaurants eating almond
cookies, sipping tea with spoons and spoons of sugar.
Popcorn and coffee was dinner. When I fainted
from migraine in the grocery store, a Portuguese
man above me mouthed: "No breakfast." He gave me
orange juice and chocolate bars. The color red
sprang into relief singing Wagner's *Walküre*.
Entire tribes gyrated and drummed in my head.
I learned the samba from a Brazilian man
so tiny, so festooned with glitter I was certain
that he slept inside a filigreed, Fabergé egg.
No one at the door: no salesmen, Mormons, meter

readers, exterminators, no Harriet Tubman,
no one. Red notes sounding in a grey trolley town.

—*Elizabeth Alexander*

Capitalist Poem #5

I was at the 7–11.
I ate a burrito.
I drank a Slurpee.
I was tired.
It was late, after work—washing dishes.
The burrito was good.
I had another.

I did it every day for a week.
I did it every day for a month.

To cook a burrito you tear off the plastic wrapper.
You push button #3 on the microwave.
Burritos are large, small, or medium.
Red or green chili peppers.
Beef or bean or both.
There are 7–11's all across the nation.

On the way out I bought a quart of beer for $1.39.
I was aware of the social injustice

in only the vaguest possible way.

—*Campbell McGrath*

At the Navajo Monument Valley
Tribal School

the football field rises
to meet the mesa. Indian boys
gallop across the grass, against

the beginning of their body.
On those Saturday afternoons,
unbroken horses gather to watch

their sons growing larger
in the small parts of the world.
Everyone is the quarterback.

There is no thin man in a big hat
writing down all the names
in two columns: winners and losers.

This is the eternal football game,
Indians versus Indians. All the Skins
in the wooden bleachers fancydancing,

stomping red dust straight down
into nothing. Before the game is over,
the eighth-grade girls' track team

comes running, circling the field,
their thin and brown legs echoing
wild horses, wild horses, wild horses.

—*Sherman Alexie*

AFTERWORD
Excerpt, Introduction

O America! how I thirst for you to shine
    & swirl in peace
        on your tiny globe
            out on the arm of a Spiral Galaxy
                we call the Milky Way

        swathed in a sheath of glowing gas
        100,000 light years across!

I am singing you America
I am singing your wilderness
your smoggy cities, your art
           & your wild creativity!
I am singing your crazy inventors
I sing the Hula Hoop & the Harley Hog & the oil of Hopper

& I am singing your schisms & controversies
O Nation, Vast & Seething
Day & Night & Dream!

War and secrecy
    make writing America
        a twistsome thing
and how many thousands of times
have I shook my head with the
        ghastly sudden knowledge
           of this and that

but how many thousands more
have I smiled at the millions
        who have made my nation a marvel.

        —*Edward Sanders*

INDEX OF FIRST LINES

221

INDEX OF POEM TITLES

226

INDEX OF POETS

PERMISSIONS

Every effort has been made to contact copyright holders for the material used in this book. The editor regrets if any omissions or errors have occurred, and will correct them in future editions of this book.

Alexander, Elizabeth: "Boston Year," from *The Venus Hottentot*, © 1990 Elizabeth Alexander. Reprinted by permission of the author.

Alexie, Sherman: "At the Navajo Monument Valley Tribal School," reprinted from *The Business of Fancydancing*, © 1992 by Sherman Alexie. Reprinted by permission of Hanging Loose Press.

Alvarez, Julia: "Queens, 1963," from *The Other Side/El Otro Lado*. Copyright © 1995 by Julia Alvarez. Published by Plume Penguin, an imprint of Dutton, a division of Penguin USA and originally in hardcover by Dutton Signet. Reprinted by permission of Susan Bergholz Literary Services, New York. All rights reserved.

Alvin, Dave: "Spiderman Versus the Kachinas," from *Any Rough Times Are Now Behind You*. Reprinted by permission of the author.

Ammons, A. R.: "First Carolina Said-Song," from *Collected Poems, 1951–1971* by A. R. Ammons. Copyright © 1972 by A. R. Ammons. Used by permission of W. W. Norton & Company, Inc.

Becker, Robin: "Community Garden, Sixth Street and Avenue B," from *The Horse Fair*, by Robin Becker, © 2000. Reprinted by permission of the University of Pittsburgh Press.

Berryman, John: "American Lights, Seen from off Abroad" from *Collected Poems: 1937–1971* by John Berryman. Copyright © 1989 by Kate Donahue Berryman. Reprinted by permission of Farrar, Straus and Giroux, LLC.

Bishop, Elizabeth: "Invitation to Miss Marianne Moore" and "Florida" from *The Complete Poems: 1927–1979* by Elizabeth Bishop. Copyright © 1979, 1983 by Alice Helen Methfessel. Reprinted by permission of Farrar, Straus and Giroux, LLC.

Bishop, John Peale: "O Pioneers!" reprinted by permission of Scribner, an imprint of Simon & Schuster Adult Publishing Group, from *The Collected Poems of John Peale Bishop*, edited by Allen Tate. Copyright © 1948 by Charles Scribner's Sons; copyright renewed © 1976.

Bly, Robert: "Sleet Storm on the Merritt Parkway," from *The Light Around the Body* by Robert Bly. Copyright © 1967 by Robert Bly. Copyright renewed 1985 by Robert Bly. Reprinted by permission of HarperCollins Publishing, Inc.

Brooks, Gwendolyn: "We Real Cool" by Gwendolyn Brooks, reprinted by permission of The Estate of Gwendolyn Brooks.

Browne, Michael Dennis: "Iowa" from *The Wife of Winter* by Michael Dennis Browne. Copyright © 1970 by Michael Dennis Browne. Reprinted by permission of the author.

Bukowski, Charles: "vegas," from *Burning in Water, Drowning in Flame* by Charles Bukowski. Copyright © 1963, 1964, 1965, 1966, 1967, 1968, 1974 by Charles Bukowski. Reprinted by permission of HarperCollins Publishers, Inc.

Carruth, Hayden: "In Georgetown," from *Scrambled Eggs & Whiskey: Poems, 1991–1995*. Copyright © 1996 by Hayden Carruth. Reprinted by permission of Copper Canyon Press, P.O. Box 271, Port Townsend, WA 98368–0271.

ABOUT THE AUTHOR

Carmela Ciuraru is the editor of the anthologies *First Loves: Poets Introduce the Essential Poems That Captivated and Inspired Them* and *Beat Poets*. She lives in New York City.